Making Je With Beads For Passionate Beginners

Maisiej .X Powersk

Crafting and beading have positive developmental effects

Your children will gain developmentally from making crafts and using beads. Spending time on both traditional crafts and bead crafts is beneficial for children of all ages. Making time for creativity is essential for your child's development, education, and learning whether you're at home or in the classroom.

Children constantly develop their social, motor, and cognitive abilities as they play and explore; these abilities will help them as they grow up as they study, work, and interact with others.

Supporting your children as they practice their talents can be extremely beneficial to their growth in a variety of ways, enabling them to swiftly absorb and put into practice the essential abilities they will use in all they do.

Here are some key developmental advantages of beading and making for kids that help them to hone and develop their most crucial abilities.

Skills with the Hands

In almost all cases, arts and crafts provide young children with wonderful opportunities to refine their fine motor skills and increase their manual dexterity. Improving these skills is a great approach to increase independence and confidence because we use our hands so much in everything we do every day.

performing things like:

maintaining a paintbrush

Pencil

forming cuts

Bead stranding

All demand fine motor coordination, thus they encourage kids to practice and improve these abilities.

The larger objects that are easier for very young children to wield utilizing the "three-jaw chuck grasp" are paintbrushes, thought markers, modeling clay, and larger beads. Activities requiring more precise manipulation, such making bracelets or designs with smaller beads, can help older kids improve their "pincer grasp."

Creativity

A child's imagination is greatly stimulated by art, craft, and beadwork, which gives them the freedom to explore and express their creativity anyway they wish. As a result, they are inspired to consider their preferences and try out a variety of hues and materials.

As children are encouraged to come up with fresh methods to discuss their work, parents may help children's language development by encouraging them to talk about their creative choices. Their learning to express oneself clearly—a skill that is essential to how successfully they connect with others—involves learning new descriptive and emotive terminology.

Cognitive Abilities

Making designs out of beads, picking out beads for a bracelet, or choosing what to construct for a craft project are all excellent projects for kids to work on their cognitive skills.

They use planning and problem-solving abilities that they will need later in life as they choose the materials to use, the design of their product, and the colors and patterns they choose. PBS Parents observed that engaging in craft activities helps improve a child's critical thinking abilities, which are essential for making wise decisions.

Social-communication abilities

Parents can aid in their child's development of critical social and communication skills by organizing craft projects that kids can do with their friends or siblings. Children can learn how to form bonds with others, deal with social circumstances, and exhibit admiration for other people's work by practicing sharing resources with other kids and showing appreciation for their effort.

They can improve their language and develop their ability to express themselves by discussing their work with one another and stating which colors or patterns they prefer. Children who share ideas while crafting might learn to respect others' choices as well as find fresh sources of inspiration and ideas for themselves.

Coordinating bilaterally

We practice bilateral coordination every day in practically everything we do. This is the act of using both hands at once to execute activities. The majority of necessary tasks require both hands to move properly and cooperatively, from tying shoelaces to opening objects to operating a computer.

For young children, craft projects are the ideal method to give them some early practice with this since tasks like cutting paper with scissors, gluing objects together, and threading beads all require the use of both hands. Parents may encourage kids to spend hours developing and perfecting this crucial skill by helping them discover something enjoyable and engrossing to do.

Visual-motor abilities

As kids learn to reproduce what they see on paper through projects that include sketching or painting specific objects, their visual motor abilities can be developed. As their visual-motor skills are improved, this enables kids to further develop other crucial abilities like handwriting. These exercises can help kids improve their fine motor control by encouraging them to use their paintbrush or pencil more precisely so they can write or draw more clearly.

Both beading and crafting are fantastic ways to help kids learn the fundamental skills they need to succeed in life, and these hobbies are special in that they help kids become more capable in a variety of domains. Children's fine motor skills are encouraged to develop through the use of arts and crafts supplies like paintbrushes, crayons, beads, and modeling clay, which enables them to move objects more precisely.

This helps kids build the physical strength, manual dexterity, and bilateral coordination that are necessary for boosting their independence and self-esteem. Children can also hone their problem-solving and decision-making abilities by organizing slightly more complicated projects, such as selecting designs and colors for beaded jewelry. Talking about these projects with kids helps them expand their vocabulary and improve their communication abilities.

Contents

CHAPTER 1

GETTING
∽ STARTED ∾

In this chapter you will learn about the various types of beads, tools, and stringing options available for making bead jewelry. You won't need everything mentioned, but over time you can refer back to this list and add more to your jewelry-making supplies. Many different designs can be made with a minimal investment and just a few items. You will find a resource list at the end of the book with suggested retailers and producers. If you prefer to shop locally so you can see and touch the materials before you buy, check your area for crafting stores or for independently owned bead shops. In general, independent stores and online retailers will offer the highest quality materials and tools.

TYPES OF BEADS

From the simplest clay beads to the most intricate lampwork beads, the range of beads available for creating jewelry is endless. Making bead jewelry lets you play with texture and color in a fun, easy, and affordable way. You can create art and express your style at the same time with beads!

Crystal Beads // Crystal beads are made from leaded glass and are often faceted, resulting in a beautiful light-reflecting quality. Swarovski is the most popular brand of crystal beads.

Gemstone Beads // Gemstone beads are made from genuine semiprecious stones, which give them unique physical characteristics that can only come from nature. They come in a wide selection of colors and are sometimes dyed. Precious stones can also be made into beads, but these are rare and very expensive.

Fire-Polished Beads // Fire-polished beads are faceted glass beads with a unique sparkly shine that is achieved by refiring the finished beads.

Pressed Glass Beads (also referred to as Czech Glass Beads) // **Pressed glass beads are made with molten glass rods that are pressed into molds. They are available in a wide variety of shapes and finishes, and can be made with recessed detail.**

Lampwork Beads // **Lampwork beads are individually handmade using glass that is heated with a flame. The glass reaches a molten state and is then shaped into its design. The fluidity of the glass while it is being worked allows for wonderful detail and texture in the beads.**

Metal Beads // Metal beads can be great accents and add a whole new dimension to your jewelry designs—for example, when pairing copper with deep blue beads or silver with a pastel color palette.

Freshwater Pearls // Freshwater pearls are formed by mussels. The pearls come in a wide variety of colors and sizes, and their shapes are usually (though not always) somewhat irregular looking. The varying shapes of freshwater pearls give them a uniquely attractive character.

Crystal Pearls // Crystal pearls are faux pearls made with a leaded crystal center, coated with a smooth, natural-looking finish. They are available in a variety of attractive shapes, sizes, and colors.

Seed Beads // Seed beads are small glass beads that are made in a wide variety of shapes, sizes, and finishes. The most widely sold and used seed beads are Czech and Japanese made. The Japanese seed beads are generally more uniform in size and shape. The Czech beads have more of a varied look from bead to bead. The larger the size number, the smaller the bead is; for example, 4 is larger than 8.

Spacer Beads // Spacer beads are small beads used as accents between larger beads in your jewelry designs. Spacer beads are usually simple in appearance. Spacers help create patterns in your jewelry, to make your pieces extra special without distracting from the design.

Bugle Beads // Bugle beads are tube-shaped glass beads that come in a variety of lengths and are longer than regular seed beads, but sized proportionately to coordinate with them.

Bead Caps // **Bead caps can add extra panache to your beads, acting as a decorative accent. You can use them at one or both ends of a bead.**

BEAD SHAPES

Beads come in many different shapes. You can mix and match them to your liking or keep similar beads together, depending on the look you are going for. Many bead holes are fairly uniform in size and will fit a variety of stringing materials and wire; however, some seed beads have smaller holes and need to be strung with nylon and other thin stringing materials. Large hole beads are available for working with cord or thicker stringing materials.

Briolette

Coin

Cube

Faceted

Heishi

Rondelle

Round

Tear Drop

BEAD STRINGING MATERIALS

There are many different types of jewelry stringing material to choose from when making a piece. Important things to consider are the size of your bead holes in relation to the thread and strength of the material. The information here will help you decide which stringing material is right for your project.

◆ Braided Thread // You can use this with seed beads as well as larger beads. Braided threads do not easily fray, making them easy to thread into a needle. These threads will not stretch or tangle—more plusses that make them easy to work with. FireLine braided thread is durable and works well for beads with sharp edges such as crystal beads. Beadalon braided thread is thermally bonded, making it smooth and colorfast.

◆ Elastic Cord // Used for making jewelry that stretches, elastic cord does not need a clasp to finish off and can simply be knotted. You can use this with many different sizes of beads, except for small hole seed beads.

◆ Hemp and Cotton Cord // Unwaxed hemp and cotton cord are great for making beaded or knotted jewelry pieces where you prefer the look and feel of a softer material that is not silky. They are available in a variety of colors.

◆ Beading Jewelry Wire // A very strong material made up of several strands of stainless steel wire coated with nylon, this stringing material is different from the heavier wire used in wirework. You will want to choose a size that will fit the smallest holes of the beads in your project. Beading jewelry wire is available in a variety of colors, which is important if you are using translucent beads, or if part of your wire will be left exposed. You will then want to choose a color that complements your beads. It is not necessary to use a needle with beading jewelry wire. Crimp tubes are the most secure option to close off clasps when using beading jewelry wire for a piece.

◆ Leather Cord // You will want to use beads with larger than normal holes when working with leather cord. A needle is not usually needed.

◆ Memory Wire // This is a very strong material that retains its shape like a Slinky. It is great for making wrap bracelets and chokers. You will need special memory wire cutters to cut memory wire as it will mar regular wire cutters. You can use memory wire with various bead sizes except for small-hole seed beads and some pearls.

◆ Nylon Beading Thread // This is good for working with seed beads, which are lighter weight than other beads. Nymo is a popular brand of nylon thread; it is a strong single-stranded thread that is good for weaving and working with seed beads. Nymo is available in a variety of colors and sizes and is easier to work with if lightly coated with beeswax before using. Size B Nymo thread will fit most seed beads and is a great size to start with. Silamide is a stronger two-ply thread that is pre-waxed and also available in various colors.

♦ Ribbon // You can use pretty much any type of narrow ribbon to string beads, provided that the beads have large enough holes.

♦ Silk Bead Cord // Silk thread is traditionally used in stringing pearls and also works well for other beads with smooth holes; it is available in a variety of colors and sizes.

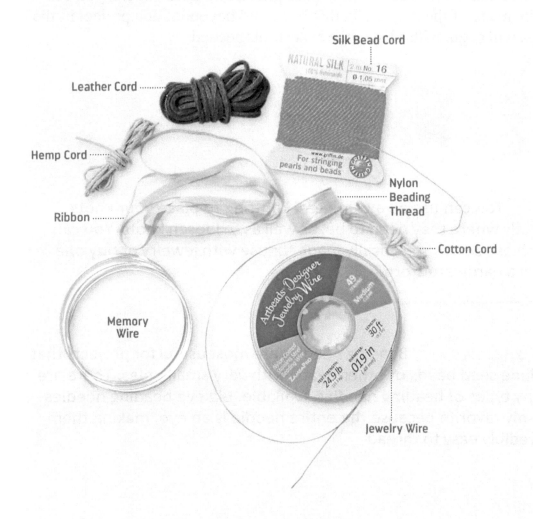

Leather Cord ....

Silk Bead Cord

NATURAL SILK | 2 m No. 16
100% Polyamid | Ø 1.05 mm

www.griffin.de
For stringing
pearls and beads

Hemp Cord ....

Ribbon ....

Nylon
Beading
Thread

.... Cotton Cord

Memory
Wire

Artbeads Designer
Jewelry Wire

49
Medium

Volcan-Coated
Stainless Steel
Beading Wire
Zaxxon Pax

TEST STRENGTH
24.9 lb
(11 kg)

DIAMETER
.019 in
(.48 mm)

LENGTH
30 ft
(9.1 m)

Jewelry Wire

MUST-HAVE TOOLS

Bead jewelry making requires very few tools. I've listed the most important items here, but even these are not all necessary. With just two pairs of chain nose pliers, round nose pliers, and flush cutters, you could make many of the projects in this book and beyond. Each project in the book will begin with a list of the exact tools needed.

Awl // You can use an awl in bead knotting to place your knots exactly where they need to be, as well as to loosen knots. You can purchase an awl specifically made for use with jewelry or buy one from a hardware store.

Beading Needles // Beading needles are most useful for projects that include seed beads or other beads with very small holes. There are many types of beading needles available. Big eye beading needles are my favorite because the entire needle is an eye, making them incredibly easy to thread.

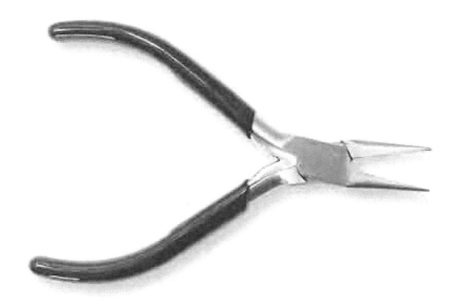

Chain Nose Pliers // These pliers are essential for working with wire and head pins, as well as opening and closing jump rings. The jaws have a smooth surface, which will prevent the wire from becoming scratched as you work with it. It is useful to have two pairs of chain nose pliers for opening and closing jump rings; one pair to hold the jump ring in place and the other to open and close it.

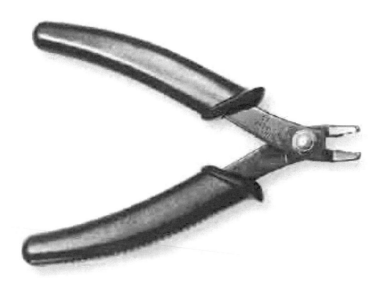

Crimping Pliers // **Crimping pliers are used to secure crimp tubes, placed at the end of a string of beads, to keep them from falling off the beading material. For a more polished look, you can hide crimp tubes inside a crimp bead using these pliers. Or, depending on the look you want, you may prefer to use the crimp tubes alone.**

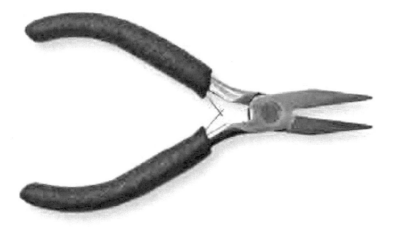

Flat Nose Pliers // **You can use flat nose pliers to create right angles in wire. You can also use them to straighten bent wires, and to open and close jump rings.**

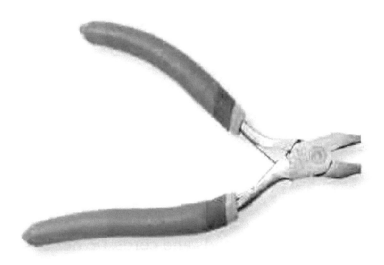

Flush Cutters // Used to cut jewelry wire and head pins, flush cutters are flat on one side, allowing for a close cut. If you can splurge on just one tool, buy the best flush cutters you can afford. It is frustrating to work with cutters that are not sharp enough to cut cleanly. There are very good cutters available (for less than $15) through the online retailers I list at the end of the book.

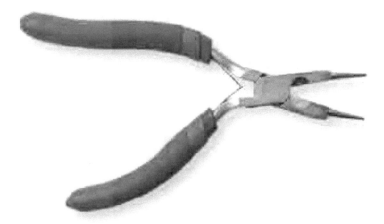

Round Nose Pliers // You can use these to create curves and loops in wire work. The jaws of these pliers are tapered and smooth, so that you can make smaller or larger loops depending on where you place your wire.

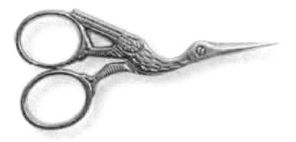

Small Scissors // Use these for cutting threads and cords. Do not use scissors to cut wire.

NICE-TO-HAVE TOOLS

You can get by without these supplies, but they can be helpful to have, making your work a little easier.

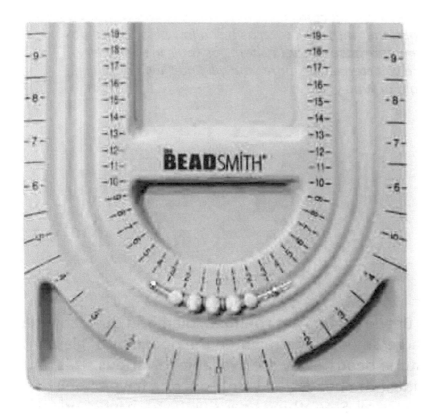

Bead Board // A bead board or work-in-progress board has compartments to hold various types of beads, as well as a U-shaped channel to lay out a necklace, earring, or bracelet design. The flocked surface keeps beads from sliding around. Bead boards are available with covers so that you can travel with your project.

Bead Mat // A bead mat does not have channels like a bead board but provides a flat textured surface that will prevent beads from rolling while you are working with them. It is helpful for laying out different colors and designs.

> **TIP:** *Create your own bead mat by lining a small cookie sheet, or other container, with a towel to keep beads from rolling around while you are working with them. Keeping a towel at the bottom of a container will*

allow you to move your project from room to room. If you want to take it on trips, use a container with a lid, such as a shallow plastic tote box. Personally, I often repurpose everyday items as tools in my jewelry making; the more you create, the more you will find "jewelry-making tools" in plain sight around you!

Bead Reamer // Bead reamers are rounded, diamond dust–covered files used to enlarge, smooth, or straighten the openings of glass, pearl, and gemstone beads. They are available in various sizes and will come in handy if the beads you want to string have openings that are a little too small. Smoothing beads with sharp inner edges, such as crystal beads, will prevent the edges from wearing down or breaking the stringing material. Occasionally a bead will not line up correctly; use this to straighten its hole. For genuine pearls, there are extra fine bead reamers designed to fit into smaller holes and remove less material, allowing the hole to be enlarged more gradually.

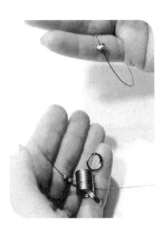

Bead Stopper // A bead stopper is a special spring that you can attach to the end of your stringing material to prevent beads from falling off while you are stringing them. If you need to put a piece aside before it is finished, the bead stopper will ensure your project doesn't fall apart, so you won't have to restring runaway beads. Though not strictly necessary, it is helpful to have three or more bead stoppers on hand, especially for projects with multiple strands.

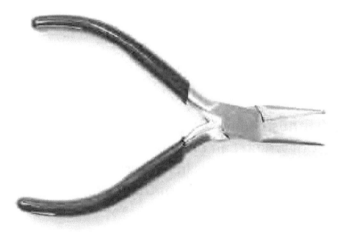

Bent Chain Nose Pliers // These work similarly to regular chain nose pliers—the difference is that they can get into tight, hard-to-reach places.

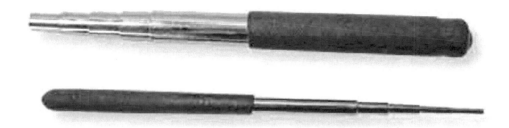

Mandrel // Mandrels are used to bend wire into curved shapes—for example, to make jump rings and curve head pins for earring wires.

Nylon Jaw Pliers // These are flat nose pliers with jaws that are covered by small blocks of nylon, which can be replaced once worn out. Nylon pliers are used to smooth out kinks in jewelry wire and to create spirals from wire with little to no marring of the wire.

FINDINGS

Think of findings as the mortar that holds bricks together in a building. Findings enable you to link parts of your jewelry together, add charms, close a bracelet, and much more. You will learn how to make some of your own findings in chapter 6.

Jump Rings // You will find jump rings invaluable in bead jewelry making. They are used to attach clasps in necklaces and bracelets, as well as charms, and to connect different parts of your designs in all types of jewelry.

Head Pins and Eye Pins // Head pins and eye pins are 2" or longer lengths of wire that you can use to add surprisingly sophisticated elements to bead jewelry. Use head pins to make charms from beads, as well as to make earring wires. Eye pins are similar to head pins but have a small loop so you can use them to connect links in necklaces and bracelets, or attach a charm with a dangle. Head pins can have a plain flat end, a small ball shape, or a fancy decorative element.

Bracelet and Necklace Closures // There are several options of closure style for bracelets and necklaces. The S-hook clasp is the simplest. A lobster clasp opens and closes with a spring mechanism and connects to your piece with a jump ring. Toggle clasps have a T-shaped bar and ring that fit together. Barrel clasps are made of two threaded parts that are twisted closed. The bracelet and necklace projects in this book will specify the types of closures needed.

Crimp Tubes // These tubes are used to secure the ends of your beading jewelry wire so that your beads won't fall off and your clasps stay on.

Crimp Beads // Optional, depending on the look you want for your piece, crimp beads are decorative covers that close over crimp tubes so they look like regular beads.

Clamshell Bead Tips // Bead tips are used at the end of a beaded strand to attach jump rings and clasps. These work well with silk, cotton, or hemp cord, and styles of chain with links that are too small for a jump ring.

Earring Findings // There are various types of earring components to hold the decorative elements of your earrings in place. Components include earring posts and backs, wire hoops, earring wires, and chandelier findings. The earring projects in this book will specify any earring findings needed.

Beginner Essentials Shopping List

In addition to your beads and stringing materials of choice, here is a list of what you'll need to get started with your bead jewelry making.

❑ Chain Nose Pliers

❑ Flat Nose Pliers

❑ Round Nose Pliers

❑ Flush Cutters

Note: For any projects that require two pairs of chain nose pliers, you can use flat nose pliers for one pair.

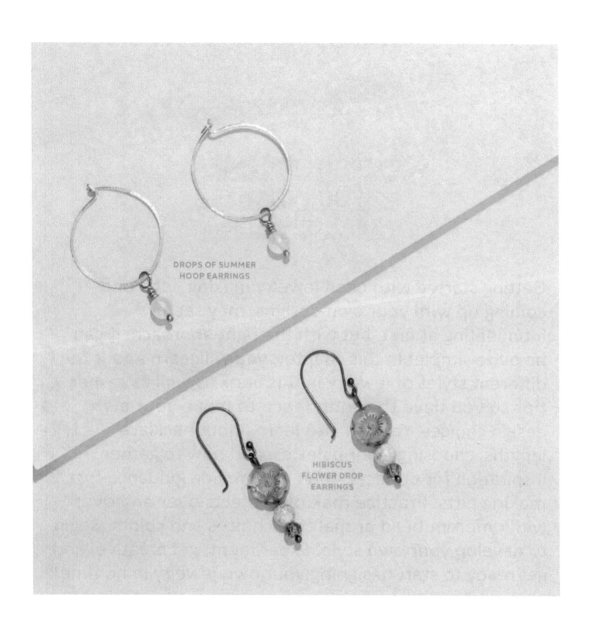

DROPS OF SUMMER
HOOP EARRINGS

HIBISCUS
FLOWER DROP
EARRINGS

CHAPTER 2

DESIGNING
∽YOUR OWN ∽
BEAD JEWELRY

Getting started with bead jewelry making, let alone coming up with your own designs, may seem intimidating at first, but with the right approach, it can be quite simple! In this chapter, you will learn about the different styles of jewelry in this book as well as garner tips so you have the confidence to make your own design choices. You will also learn about necklace lengths, choosing color palettes, and how to gather inspiration for projects, and I will provide guidance for making gifts. Practice making projects over and over with different bead or material choices and colors. Begin to develop your own style. Experiment, get creative, and get ready to start designing your own jewelry in no time!

FIND YOUR STYLE

If thinking about the myriad of tools, bead types, and jewelry styles is making your head spin, I can relate, but bead jewelry making is incredibly creative and rewarding. The first goal of this book is to teach you how to make gorgeous jewelry you will love to wear and gift to your favorite people. You'll find jewelry projects in three general style categories. Once you are comfortable with the techniques you've learned and start to get a sense of the styles you like, have fun experimenting and playing with different colors and textures. I hope you have a great time making jewelry that expresses your own unique style and the artistic looks you want to create!

Elegant // These pieces are classic yet have a whimsical feel expressed through an unusual color or material.
* Ombre Bracelet
* Coral Knotted Bracelet
* Wrapped Briolette Pendant

Playful // These projects have unexpected details, such as mixed techniques or colors and are a bit bolder in style than the other categories.
* Cerulean Treasure Necklace
* Candy Dreams Bracelet
* Peachy Tassel Necklace
* Little Owl Necklace
* Chevron Fringe Earrings
* Pink Lotus Necklace
* I'm Charmed Bracelet
* Dappled Light Necklace
* Radiant in Red Earrings

Delicate // **These pieces are understated and delicate in style.**
  * Walk in the City Heishi Necklace
  * Green Grass Necklace
  * Citrus on Your Wrist Bracelet

ALL THE COLORS OF THE RAINBOW

The look of the jewelry designs in this book are simply suggestions. I will give you necessary information on how to construct each piece and the materials needed. The colors and styles I chose for the different elements are based on my personal taste. Make the designs your own by changing up what you see! Try using a color wheel to come up with interesting color palettes. Color wheels feature 12 colors made up of the three primary colors: red, yellow, and blue. They can help you combine colors in ways that are pleasing to the eye and get your creativity going. Using one, I've often thought up color combinations I never even considered. Try a monochromatic (using different shades or tones of the same color) grouping of cool or warm colors. Or, use the wheel to identify contrasting but complementary colors that sit across from each other, and try a medley of these. In recent years, ombre (graduated hues of a color shading into each other from light to dark) has been a popular color style; you'll find a fun ombre bracelet project here. Color wheels are available at most arts and crafts stores. If you would like to delve deeper into this topic, you can find articles and entire books completely dedicated to the study of color theory.

NECKLACE LENGTHS

The look and feel of a necklace can vary from formal to fun and playful, depending on the materials used and the necklace length. Where exactly a necklace sits on the body when worn will vary slightly depending on the height of the person wearing it. These are the most popular necklace lengths.

Collar // This is the closest fitting necklace and is 14" or shorter.

Choker // A little bit longer than a collar at 14" to 16", this sits at or close to the collarbone.

Princess // This measures between 17" and 19" and sits below the collarbone.

Matinee // This is between 20" and 24" and sits at chest level.

Opera // This measures between 34" and 37" and typically sits around the upper abdomen or end of the rib cage.

Rope // A rope length is between 48" to 60" and can be doubled or tripled around the neck.

Multistrand // A multistrand necklace is made of strands of various attached lengths (usually three strands, sometimes more).

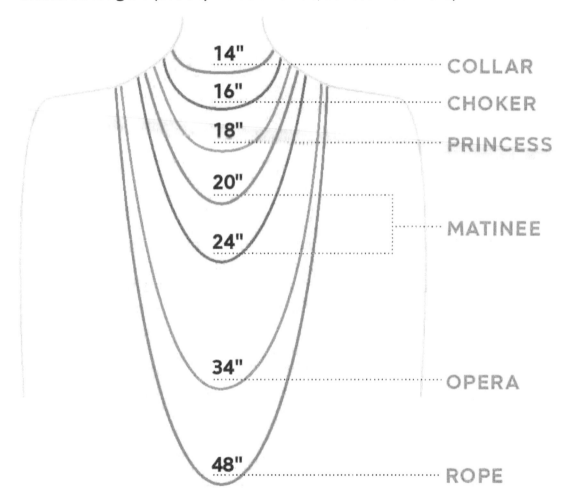

MAKING JEWELRY GIFTS

Often one of the most difficult parts of gift giving is finding something that your recipient will connect with, an item that is really "them." What better way to solve this than by making a piece of custom jewelry for your friend or loved one? You can use their favorite colors and give them something completely personalized to their style and aesthetic. Before you start creating, here are some items to consider.

Your Recipient's Style Preferences

Does the person like to wear bold colors and large pieces of jewelry, or dainty, smaller pieces? Think about the colors of clothing and accessories that your recipient normally wears and use it as a guide when creating the piece. If you are unsure of color preferences, neutral colors such as silver or gold, shades of white, ivory, gray, or blush are good choices, as they will match most any outfit.

Level of Activity

Is the gift recipient active, preferring simple pieces that don't have a lot of dangling parts? Is your piece secure—for example, with backings to keep earrings from falling out?

Metal Allergies

If possible, you will want to find out if your gift recipient has any metal allergies. You can use hypoallergenic jewelry components if you are unsure. Gold, niobium, surgical steel, and titanium are some examples of hypoallergenic metals. Nickel is commonly allergenic, so using nickel-free materials is important, too.

Pierced Ears

You will want to be sure the recipient's ears are pierced if you are considering making earrings. Clip on earrings are an option, but you will want to know if these would be worn. If in doubt, make a necklace or bracelet instead.

Gift for a Child

If the recipient is a child, check if the parents are okay with jewelry gifts. If the child is under the age of five, it may be best not to give jewelry, especially if it is something with small parts that could potentially be a choking hazard, or a necklace that could get caught on something while the child is playing.

Measurements

You will want to be sure the piece you make fits your gift recipient to avoid disappointment. You can ask someone close to the person for sizing information or create a piece that is adjustable—for example, by adding a small piece of chain to a bracelet clasp. Necklaces will fit a variety of sizes, provided they are not choker style; 18" or 24" are good sizes to go with.

GET INSPIRED!

It is useful (and fun) to keep track of visual elements that inspire you on your jewelry-making journey. I often find that I am designing in my head well before I make a piece of jewelry. I might see something in nature or architecture that catches my eye and snap a photo with my phone for later reference, or if I'm really inspired, I'll sketch it in a little notebook I carry around. Creating an inspiration board is easy and allows you to view your images whenever you are in your work space, which can really help your creativity. Use a bulletin board and simply pin on clippings from magazines or photos, as well as fabric swatches and even bead samples in plastic bags. Seeing and referring to these materials and images can be the best kind of inspiration, especially if you are a tactile person.

You can also create a convenient, online inspiration board on Pinterest, which you can keep private so that others don't see it. You can even create several boards focusing on different types of jewelry or styles. If you see an image online with colors and shapes that inspire you, save it to a Pinterest board or in a special folder you create on your computer.

BEGINNER CHEAT SHEET

1 Start with the tools listed in the Beginner Essentials Shopping List (here) and ignore the rest until you feel comfortable moving on to more challenging projects.

2 Learn how to open and close jump rings (here) and then start with the Hibiscus Flower Drop Earrings, which is the easiest jewelry piece to make in the book. If you don't want to make your own earring wires just yet, no problem; you can purchase premade earring wires. Making these earrings will give you practice with one of the most adaptable techniques in bead jewelry making: creating a simple loop (here). Knowing how to create a loop and work with jump rings opens a whole world of possibilities as far as the range of pieces you will be able to create. These two techniques will ensure that you can create more complex projects with ease.

3 Take your new skills a step further and make other types of jewelry using just the decorative bead portion from the Hibiscus Drop Earrings.

♦ **Use the simple loop bead as a charm for a necklace.** Instead of using earring wires, simply attach the decorative piece to a chain using a jump ring. You can use a premade chain, or if you're feeling ready to go further, use jump rings on the ends of a cut chain, with a lobster clasp (as described in the Peachy Tassel Necklace project).

♦ **Make longer, dangling earrings.** Use an eye pin instead of a head pin for the beaded portion of the earring. Attach an extra bead or charm onto the bottom loop with a jump ring to make a dangle.

◆ **Make a linked bead bracelet or necklace.** Follow the exact rules for making the decorative portion of an earring, except use an eye pin instead of a head pin. Make multiples of these and link them together with jump rings. You can attach a clasp as you do in the linked bead bracelet project ([here](#)), or simply size the bracelet so that it can easily slip on and off your wrist. To make a necklace, continue to make and attach looped beads until you have the length you desire. The number of items you can make after learning just two techniques is impressive—I wish I had known this when I was first starting out! Have fun with it!

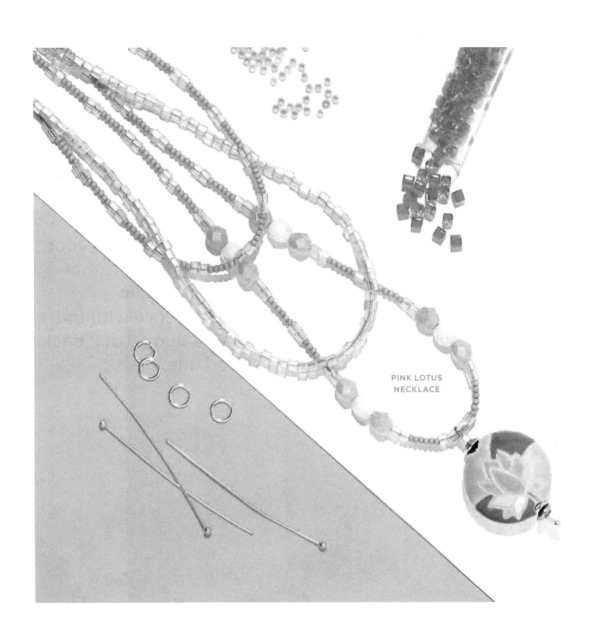

PINK LOTUS
NECKLACE

CHAPTER 3

⟡BASIC⟡
TECHNIQUES

The following basic techniques will be cornerstones in your bead jewelry making projects. These are simple skills that are used to create many different jewelry pieces, in combination or alone. You will get lots of practice with these techniques by making the projects in this book. Look back at this section for a refresher if you need one.

OPENING JUMP RINGS

This technique is probably the most basic one you will learn and also one of the most important. Jump rings are used to attach different components of your designs; if pried open, they can break, so follow these instructions carefully.

Materials **Jump rings**
Tools **2 pairs chain nose pliers**

1 Use two chain nose pliers (or another type of pliers with smooth, flat jaws). With a pair of pliers in each hand, grasp each side of the jump ring; the opening of the ring should be facing up and centered while you do this.

2 In a twisting motion, move one ring end forward and the other toward you. Do this in reverse to close the jump ring. It is important not to pull the jump rings apart at their sides, as this will weaken and possibly break the jump ring.

CRIMPING

Crimping with crimp tubes is used to secure the ends of beading jewelry wire with a clasp in necklace or bracelet projects. It can also work with some types of cord.

Materials Beading jewelry wire, crimp tubes, clasp, 2 jump rings, crimp beads (optional)
Tools Crimping pliers

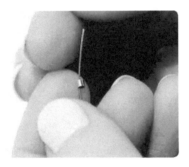

1 Thread a crimp tube onto your wire. (You can add a clasp at this point; simply make sure there is a little bit of space between the crimp tube and the clasp, so they are not touching.)

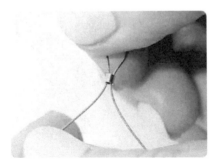

2 Push the end of your wire back through the crimp tube, forming a loop at the top. There will be a tail from the end of your wire at one side. Adjust the loop if necessary so its size is to your liking.

3 Use crimping pliers to secure the crimp tube as follows: Using the notch closer to the handle, squeeze the crimp into a figure 8 shape.

4 Separate the wire tail from the main wire by holding them as if each side is a leg.

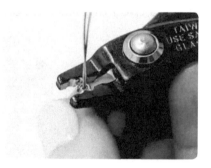

5 Using the notch closer to the tip of the pliers, squeeze the crimp tube, forming it into a U shape (you have essentially folded the tube in half).

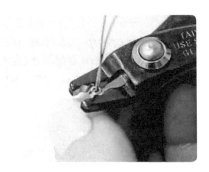

6 Use the pliers to squeeze the two sides of the U together. For a more polished finish, use the notch closer to the handle to close a crimp bead cover over the tube.

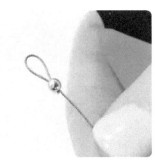

7 Using your flush cutters, trim off the excess wire, or "tail."

8 String your beads onto the jewelry wire. Repeat the crimping process on the other side, with a jump ring or loop instead of a clasp, depending on the style of clasp you used. Be sure to trim any excess wire.

TIP: *Always make sure that your crimp tubes and crimp beads are lined up as straight as possible in your pliers before closing them. Once you have closed them, you will not be able to open and reposition them.*

TYING BASIC KNOTS

When tying a knot on a cord or string, it is nearly impossible to get it exactly where you want it to be. Using this simple method, you will be able to place your knots perfectly! You can purchase an awl at your local hardware store, or, alternately, a special beading awl is available through some beading and craft stores. Both work equally well.

Materials **Beading string or cord, beads**
Tools **Awl, ruler, pencil or chalk**

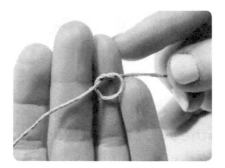

1 Tie a simple knot on the beading string, toward the top, leaving 2" to 3" of extra string above it to add a closure later.

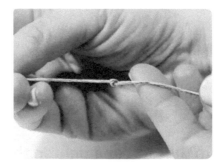

2 Pull the string to tighten the knot.

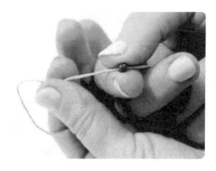

3 String on your first bead or beads.

4 Make a loose knot close to the end of your beads and tighten it around the awl. Using the awl, push the knot closer to the beads. You will find the awl makes it easier to move the knot so it will wind up right where you want it.

5 Remove the awl from the knot and tighten the knot more if needed.

6 Use a ruler to measure where you want your next knotted bead or beads to be. With a pencil, mark the spot where you would like your knot to be on your string. If working with a dark color string, use chalk.

7 Tie a loose knot close to the pencil mark. Use the awl to slide your knot over to where your pencil mark is as you did in step 4. Remove the awl from the knot and tighten the knot more if needed. Add desired number of beads. Repeat this process for each knot.

FORMING A SIMPLE LOOP

The simple loop is one of the most essential techniques in bead jewelry making. You can use it to make decorative drops for earrings, necklace charms, connected link bracelets, and necklaces.

Materials 2" head pin or eye pin, bead
Tools Flush cutters, chain nose pliers, round nose pliers

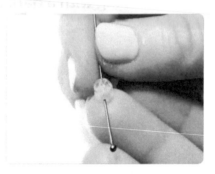

1 Place your bead or beads onto a head pin and slide it (or them) down to the bottom.

2 Using flush cutters, cut the head pin about ⅜" above the top bead.

3 With your finger or chain nose pliers, bend the remaining wire above the bead into a right angle. Make sure it is tight against the top of the bead. You can use the round nose pliers to tighten it if needed.

4 With the round nose pliers, grasp the end of the wire and rotate the pliers to make a curve.

5 Continue until you've reached the bead to form a loop.

6 If there is a gap between the loop and bead, you can use the chain nose pliers to open it (like you would a jump ring) and close it tighter.

TIP: *You can open and close the loop to attach it to a piece of jewelry, or attach it using a jump ring. Use an eye pin instead of a head pin If you are going to use the finished piece as a link in a necklace or bracelet, or if you want to dangle another bead from the bottom.*

FORMING A WRAPPED BEADED LOOP

You can use wrapped loops as bead connectors, to attach clasps, and to make charms and bead dangles for earrings and necklaces. They are particularly useful when using thinner wire since the wrap will add strength, making this style more secure than a simple wire loop.

Materials 2" head pin or eye pin, bead
Tools Round nose pliers, chain nose pliers, flush cutters

1 Thread a bead onto the head pin or eye pin.

2 With the round nose pliers, bend the wire ⅛" above the bead into a 90-degree angle.

3 Use the round nose pliers to grasp the wire at the top of the bend; wrap the wire around the top jaw of the pliers, until it forms a curve and the wire is pointing downward.

4 Move the round nose pliers to a horizontal position to finish the circle. Push the wire until it has formed a loop.

5 Hold the loop with the pliers. Using the chain nose pliers or your finger, wrap the wire end below the loop around the wire "neck" 3 times.

6 Trim off the excess wire with the flush cutters.

7 Use the chain nose pliers to flatten the end of the wire against the loops.

CHEVRON
FRINGE EARRINGS

CORAL
KNOTTED BRACELET

CERULEAN TREASURE
NECKLACE

CHAPTER 4

∽BEAD∾
STRINGING AND KNOTTING

In this section, you will learn how to string beads for bracelets, necklaces, and earrings. Some of the projects are simple and others, like the Chevron Fringe Earrings and Pink Lotus Necklace, are more complicated. The Green Grass Necklace and Coral Knotted Bracelet projects are created by knotting beads. All the projects build on the foundational techniques covered in the book.

OMBRE BRACELET

This project will allow you to apply some basic techniques, including crimping and attaching a clasp. Being an ombre design, this bracelet shades tones of color into each other. You can use the design idea pictured, or mix things up with this technique, for example, by using a series of ombre color designs. Have fun with this!

TECHNIQUES LEARNED

♦ Stringing beads

♦ Securing beads with end crimps

♦ Attaching a closure

MATERIALS

♦ 1 piece of nylon-coated stainless steel jewelry wire, 5¼" or longer, depending on wrist size

♦ 2 (2mm) crimp tubes

♦ 2 (5mm) jump rings (okay if slightly larger size)

♦ 1 (12mm) lobster clasp

♦ 10 (6mm) faceted beads

♦ 4 (8mm) faceted beads

♦ 4 (6mm) round beads

♦ 3 (9mm) faceted rondelle beads

♦ 2 (4mm) faceted beads

TOOLS

♦ Tape measure

- ◆ Flush cutters
- ◆ 2 pairs of chain nose pliers

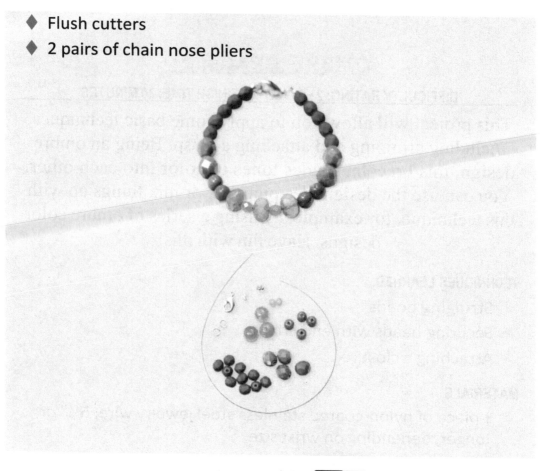

1 Use a tape measure to measure your wrist. Measure and cut the wire ½" longer.

2 (pictured above) Using the crimping pliers, attach a crimp tube (see <u>here</u>), creating a loop at one end of the jewelry wire.

3 Thread beads onto the jewelry wire in the following order: 5 (6mm) faceted beads, 2 (8mm) faceted beads, 2 (6mm) round beads, 1 (9mm) rondelle bead, 1 (4mm) faceted bead, 1 (9mm) rondelle bead, 1 (4mm) faceted bead, 1 (9mm) rondelle bead; repeat mirror image of beads on other side of bracelet, starting with 2 (6mm) round beads.

4 Attach a crimp tube and make a crimped loop at the end of the beaded wire as in step 2. Be sure to trim any excess wire.

5 Using 2 pliers, open a jump ring (see <u>here</u>); attach it and the ring portion of the clasp to one end of the bracelet. Open and attach a jump ring and the lobster clasp to the other end.

CERULEAN TREASURE NECKLACE

This chunky necklace has an interesting pattern, allowing you to mix and match small and large beads.

TECHNIQUES LEARNED

♦ Stringing beads

♦ Securing beads with end crimps

♦ Attaching a closure

MATERIALS

♦ 2 (2mm) crimp tubes

♦ 2 crimp bead covers (sized to fit 2mm crimp tubes)

♦ 4 (6mm) melon-shaped Czech glass beads

♦ 6 (6mm) metal-faceted beads

♦ 18 (4mm) round TOHO seed beads

♦ 4 (6mm) flat disk metal spacer beads

♦ 2 (8mm) faceted beads

♦ 4 (6mm) Czech glass flat disk spacer beads

♦ 3 (10mm) English-cut Czech glass beads

♦ 16" of nylon-coated, stainless steel jewelry wire

♦ 1 (8mm or larger) jump ring

♦ 1 (5mm or larger) jump ring

♦ 1 (11mm or larger) lobster clasp

TOOLS

♦ Crimping pliers

♦ 2 pairs of chain nose pliers

♦ Flush cutters

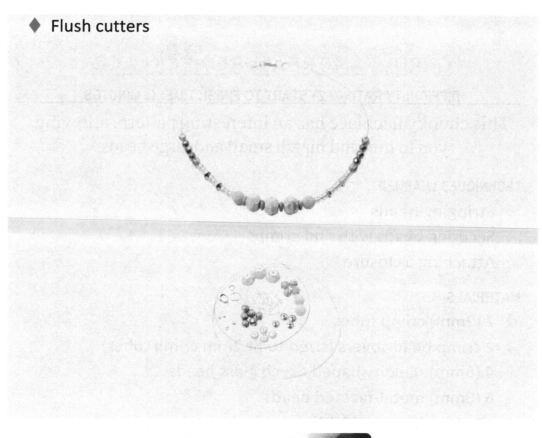

1 Using the crimping pliers, attach a crimp tube (see <u>here</u>), creating a loop at the end of the jewelry wire.

2 The loop should look like this.

3 Cover the crimp tube with a crimp bead (see <u>here</u>). Use the flush cutters to trim any excess wire.

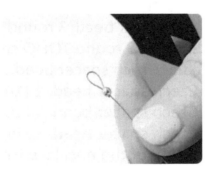

4 The finished loop with the crimp bead should look like this.

5 String 1 (6mm) melon-shaped Czech glass bead onto the jewelry wire.

6 String on the following beads: 3 (6mm) faceted metal beads, 1 (6mm) melon-shaped Czech glass bead, 3 (4mm) round TOHO seed beads, 1 (6mm) flat metal spacer bead, 3 round TOHO seed beads, 1 (6mm) flat metal spacer bead, 3 round TOHO seed beads, 1 (8mm) faceted bead, 1 (6mm) flat Czech spacer bead, 1 (10mm) English-cut Czech bead, 1 (6mm) Czech spacer bead, 1 (10mm) English-cut Czech bead, 1 (6mm) Czech spacer bead, 1 (10mm) English-cut Czech bead, 1 (6mm) Czech spacer bead. String a mirror image of the beads on the other side of the necklace from the 8mm faceted bead on (refer to the photo).

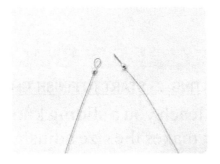

7 Finish the other end of the necklace with a crimp tube and crimp bead cover, as in steps 1 to 3. Be sure to trim any excess wire.

8 Using 2 pliers, open the 5mm jump ring (see here); attach it and a lobster clasp to the right end of the necklace. Open and attach the 8mm jump ring to the other end of the necklace.

TIP: *Increase the number of large beads in this necklace for a bolder look.*

CANDY DREAMS BRACELET

This bracelet will teach you a sliding knot technique to use as a closure, which makes the size adjustable and eliminates the need for a clasp. You can use the sliding knot closure to make necklaces as well.

TECHNIQUES LEARNED

♦ Beading with cord

♦ Making an adjustable-size sliding knot closure

♦ Stringing beads

MATERIALS

♦ Smooth suede or leather cord

♦ 18 (4mm) metal spacer beads

♦ 8 (8mm) faceted glass beads

♦ 1 (10mm) faceted glass bead

TOOLS

♦ Small scissors

♦ Ruler

1 Wrap a length of cord around your wrist and add 3" of extra length to each end, then cut.

2 **(pictured above)** String on the following beads: 3 spacer beads, 3 (8mm) beads, 3 spacer beads, 1 (8mm) bead, 1 (10mm) bead, 1 (8mm) bead, 3 spacer beads, 3 (8mm) beads, 3 spacer beads.

3 Center the beads on the cord and line up the ends of the cord.

4 Tie a loose knot about 2" from one end of the cord.

5 Slide the other cord end through the loose knot.

6 Knot this end of the cord onto the main cord leaving about 2" of cord at the end as on the previous side.

7 Slide 3 spacer beads onto each cord end.

8 Tie a knot to hold the spacer beads in place.

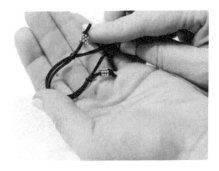

9 Your bracelet is ready! It is adjustable to fit any size wrist.

TIP: *In order to ensure that your bracelet is easy to adjust, choose a sturdy cord that is smooth. Use beads with holes that are large enough to fit the cord.*

WALK IN THE CITY HEISHI NECKLACE

The faceted beads I used for this necklace are fire-polished Czech glass beads. In general, I like to work with Czech glass beads because they not only add a little sparkle to pieces as they catch the light, but they also tend to have rich high-quality finishes. Raven's Journey is my favorite Czech glass bead manufacturer; several online retailers carry them. But, of course, you can use any type of beads you prefer.

TECHNIQUES LEARNED

- Stringing beads
- Securing beads with end crimps
- Attaching closures

MATERIALS

- 21" of nylon-coated, stainless steel jewelry wire
- 2 (2mm) crimp tubes
- 36 (3mm) faceted glass beads
- 20 (6mm) metal disk spacer beads
- 20 (4mm) faceted glass beads
- 10 (6mm) round glass beads
- 5 (8mm) rondelle beads
- 12 (8mm) shell (or other material) heishi beads
- 1 (8mm or larger) jump ring
- 1 (5mm or larger) jump ring

♦ 1 (11mm or larger) lobster clasp

TOOLS

♦ 2 bead stoppers (optional)
♦ Crimping pliers
♦ 2 pairs of chain nose pliers
♦ Flush cutters

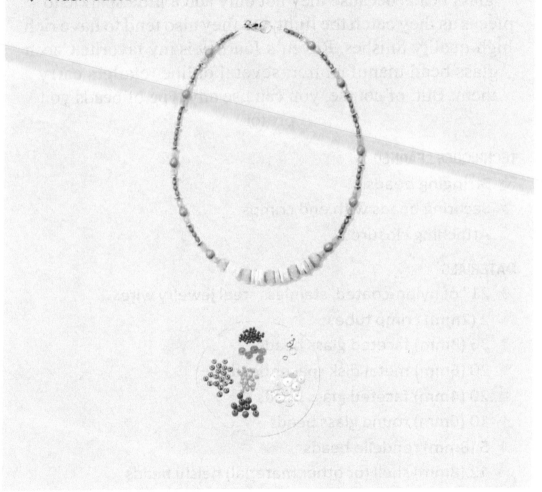

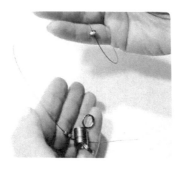

1 Attach one bead stopper about 1" from the end of the jewelry wire. If you don't have bead stoppers or prefer to close the end of your wire right away, you can attach a crimp tube (see here), creating a loop, before starting to thread on your beads.

2 Thread beads onto the jewelry wire in the patterns that follow: 3 (3mm) beads, 1 disk spacer, 1 (4mm) bead, 1 (6mm) round bead, 1 (4mm) bead, 1 disk spacer. Repeat this pattern one time. 3 (3mm) beads, 1 disk spacer. Repeat this pattern one time. 1 (4mm) bead, 1 (6mm) bead, 1 (4mm) bead, 1 disk spacer, 3 (3mm) beads, 1 disk spacer. Repeat this pattern one time. 1 (4mm) bead, 1 (6mm) bead, 1 (4mm) bead. 1 rondelle bead, 3 heishi beads. Repeat this pattern 3 times, then finish with the last rondelle bead. You will have used up all 5 rondelle and 12 heishi beads. On the other side of the necklace repeat the patterns to create a mirror image of the finished side.

3 Your necklace in progress should look like this.

4 Using the crimping pliers, attach a crimp tube (see <u>here</u>), creating a loop at the end of the jewelry wire.

5 Repeat this process on the other end of the necklace if you did not do it at the beginning.

6 Be sure to trim any excess wire if necessary.

7 Using 2 pliers, open the 5mm jump ring (see <u>here</u>); attach it and a lobster clasp to the right end of the necklace.

8 Open and attach the 8mm jump ring to the left end of the necklace.

TIP: *Using a bead stopper will prevent your beads from sliding off the wire. If you are not using one and choose not to attach a crimp tube in step 1, keep an eye and hand on the bottom end of your wire, so your beads don't fall off.*

PEACHY TASSEL NECKLACE

This pretty tassel necklace is a quick and easy project that allows you to exercise your creativity. Choose from a seemingly endless array of embroidery floss colors, or mix and match different beads and bead caps.

TECHNIQUES LEARNED

- Making a wrapped bead wire
- Working with a bead cap
- Attaching closures

MATERIALS

- 110" (about) piece of 6-ply embroidery thread
- 1 business card (or other piece of card)
- Bead cap of choice
- 1 bead of choice
- 17" of necklace chain
- 3 (4.5mm) jump rings
- 1 (12mm) lobster clasp

TOOLS

- Round nose pliers
- Flush cutters
- Chain nose pliers

1 Loop embroidery thread around a 2.9" card (I used a business card), making sure the beginning and end of the thread are aligned with the loop you create.

2 If there is extra thread at the bottom of the looped threads, trim it to align with the rest of the loop.

3 Using your fingers, make a curved bend at the end of the wire so that there is about an inch of wire on the left side.

4 Open the loop and attach the loop of thread to it.

5 With the embroidery thread placed over the wire so that it is even on either end, begin creating a wrapped loop.

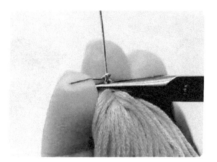

6 Hold the loop with the pliers. Using the chain nose pliers or your finger, wrap the wire end above the loop around the wire "neck" 2 to 3 times.

7 Trim off the excess wire with the flush cutters.

8 Thread the bead cap onto the wire, followed by the bead.

9 Pull down on the loop of threads so they are secured into the bead cap.

10 Bend the wire ⅛" above the bead at a 90-degree angle.

11 Using round nose pliers, make a wrapped loop above the bead (see here).

12 Wrap the wire end around the wire neck several times.

13 Cut the looped threads at the bottom.

14 Trim the bottom of the tassel so the threads are of equal length.

15 Open and attach a jump ring (see here) and the finished tassel pendant to the necklace chain.

16 Open and attach a jump ring and the lobster clasp to the right end of the necklace chain. Open and attach a jump ring to the other end.

TIP: You can vary the length of your tassels by using a different size card when wrapping your embroidery thread. Maybe try some mini tassels for a multiple tassel piece, or extra-large ones for statement pieces!

LITTLE OWL NECKLACE

This project pairs an owl-shaped bead charm with a simple bead pattern for a cute choker-length necklace. A focal bead or focal charm is the center of attention in a piece of jewelry. Think of it as the star in a Broadway show and the other beads as supporting cast members. You can create your entire design around the focal bead by choosing harmonious colors and styles for the smaller beads.

TECHNIQUES LEARNED

♦ Making a simple looped beaded charm with a head pin
♦ Securing beads with crimps
♦ Attaching closures

MATERIALS

♦ 1 (2") head pin
♦ 7 (9mm) faceted rondelle beads
♦ 1 owl-shaped focal bead
♦ 4 (6mm) faceted beads
♦ 16" piece of nylon-coated stainless steel jewelry wire
♦ 12 (6mm) pearl beads
♦ 12 (6mm) round beads
♦ 2 crimp tubes
♦ 2 crimp cover beads
♦ 2 (5mm or slightly larger) jump rings
♦ 1 (11mm or slightly larger) lobster clasp

TOOLS

- ◆ Flush cutters
- ◆ Round nose pliers
- ◆ Crimping pliers
- ◆ 2 chain nose pliers

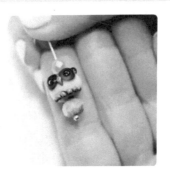

MAKE THE FOCAL CHARM

1 Thread 1 (9mm) rondelle bead, 1 focal bead, and 1 (6mm) round bead onto a head pin. Using flush cutters, cut the head pin about ¾" above the top bead.

2 Bend the remaining wire into a right angle and use round nose pliers to create a loop.

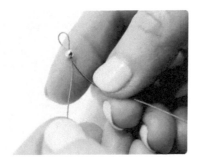

MAKE THE NECKLACE

1 Using the crimping pliers, attach a crimp tube and crimp bead cover to one end of the jewelry wire (see <u>here</u>) leaving a loop. Snip off the excess wire with the flush cutters.

2 String the beads onto the jewelry wire in this pattern: 1 (6mm) pearl, 1 (6mm) faceted bead, 1 (6mm) pearl, 1 (6mm) round bead, 1 (9mm) rondelle, 1 (6mm) round bead. Repeat once. Then, follow with this pattern: 1 (6mm) pearl, 1 (9mm) round bead, 1 rondelle, 1 (6mm) round bead, 1 (6mm) pearl.

3 String on the focal charm.

4 Repeat step 2, this time stringing on the same beads as the other side, in a mirror image.

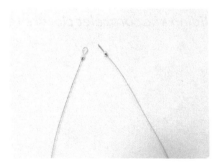

5 Attach the other crimp tube and crimp bead cover to the end of the necklace as in step 1.

6 Using 2 pliers, open a jump ring (see <u>here</u>); attach it and a lobster clasp to the right end of the necklace.

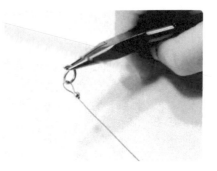

7 Open and attach a jump ring to the left end of the necklace.

TIP: *Try making this design with a leather cord and beads that have larger holes. Use the sliding knot bracelet closure technique <u>here</u>.*

GREEN GRASS NECKLACE

The cool greens of the beads and cord in this necklace complement each other, resulting in a pleasant monochromatic look. Try changing up the design by using your favorite color or match the bead colors to a special outfit. You can also play around with the design by adding more beads or changing their spacing.

TECHNIQUES LEARNED

♦ Knotting beads

♦ Making a pendant with a head pin

♦ Making a clasp with jewelry wire

MATERIALS

♦ 1 teardrop-shaped bead

♦ 30 (2mm) seed beads

♦ 1 (2") head pin

♦ 48" of hemp jewelry cord

♦ 2 pieces (4" long each) of 24-gauge jewelry wire

♦ Glue (Power Grab by Loctite is a good brand)

♦ 2 (4.5mm) jump rings

♦ 1 (12mm) lobster clasp

TOOLS

♦ Awl

♦ Chain nose pliers

♦ Flush cutters

- ◆ Flat nose pliers
- ◆ Scissors

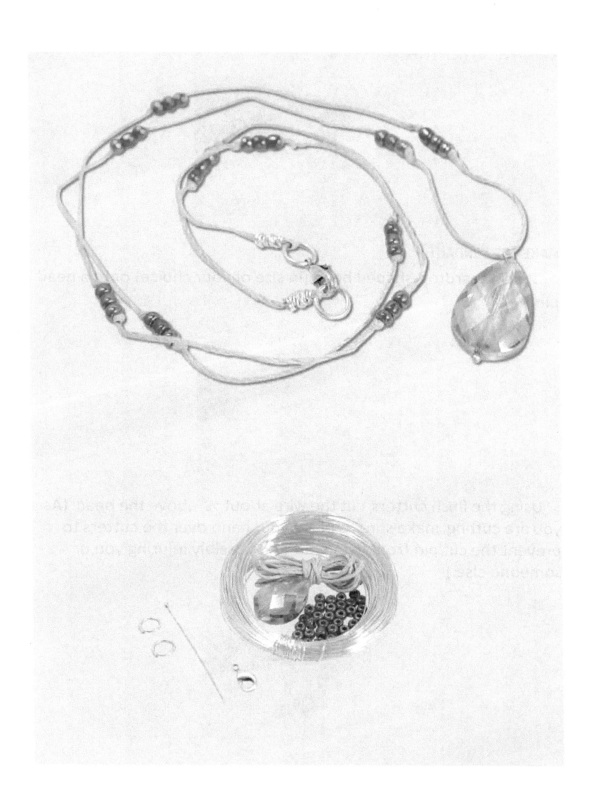

MAKE THE PENDANT

1 Slide a teardrop-shaped bead (in size of your choice) onto a head pin.

2 Using the flush cutters, cut the wire about ⅜" above the bead. (As you are cutting, make sure to place your hand over the cutters to prevent the cut pin from flying out and possibly injuring you or someone else.)

3 With the tip of the round nose pliers, grasp the head pin wire, just above the bead, and bend it at a right angle. (If the head pin is flexible enough, you can use your fingers.)

4 Grasp the end of the wire with the round nose pliers. With a rotating motion, curve the wire around the pliers, in the opposite direction, until you reach the other side of where the right angle was, making a simple loop. Straighten the curve so that it aligns with the pin.

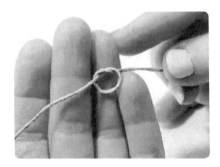

MAKE THE NECKLACE
1 Tie a knot about 3" away from one end of the cord.

2 Slide 3 of the seed beads up to the knot.

3 Tie a loose knot, close to the third bead. Using the awl, slide the knot over until it is right next to the bead (see <u>here</u>).

4 Remove the awl and tighten the knot.

5 Using a ruler, measure 2½" from the knot; mark the cord. Tie another knot close to the pencil mark. Slide the knot over with the awl, if necessary.

6 Repeat steps 2 to 5, until you have five groups of three beads; each group will be 2½" apart.

7 Slide the teardrop pendant onto the cord.

8 On the right side of the cord, continue to knot the remaining beads in groups of three, until you have made five sets of three beads. You can check your work by lining up the pencil marks and making sure the beads on the right and left sides of your necklace are aligned.

9 Fold over one end of the necklace cord, into a very small loop, ensuring that there is a 1" space between the very first knot and the beginning of the loop.

10 Take a 4" piece of jewelry wire and fold the end of it over the base of the loop, squeezing it closed and letting about 1" of one end align with the cord. Place a dab of glue on the cord where the wire meets it. Wrap the jewelry wire around the cord, covering up the 1" of wire. If there is any wire left, wrap it in the opposite direction, over your original wraps.

11 Trim any excess wire with the flush cutters.

12 Use chain nose pliers to squeeze the end of the wire so that it is flush against the wrapped wire.

13 Repeat this process on the other cord end, again making sure that the base of your loop is 1" away from the first knotted group of beads.

14 Using 2 pliers, open a jump ring (see here) and attach it to the left cord loop. Trim off any excess cord with scissors.

15 Using 2 pliers, open a jump ring and attach it and the lobster clasp to the right cord loop.

16 Your finished clasp will look something like this.

TIP: *There is no need for the wrapping to be neat or tidy; a natural look is what you're going for here. Like an artist with a paintbrush, or the difference between one person's signature and another's, the way you wrap the cord and how it looks can be part of your unique jewelry-making style.*

CORAL KNOTTED BRACELET

This project expands on the knotting method introduced in the Green Grass Necklace project. You will find that using an awl makes knotting beads incredibly easy and precise.

TECHNIQUES LEARNED

♦ Knotting beads

♦ Attaching closures with clamshell crimp connectors

MATERIALS

♦ 16 to 20 (8mm) beads, depending on wrist size

♦ 20" of 1.05mm silk cord with a pre-attached needle

♦ 2 (7.3 × 3.7 × 3.3mm, or slightly larger) clamshell crimp connectors

♦ 1 (8mm) jump ring (size can vary slightly)

♦ 1 (12mm) jump ring (size can vary slightly)

♦ Glue (Power Grab by Loctite is a good brand)

♦ 1 (12mm) lobster clasp

TOOLS

♦ Awl

♦ 2 pairs of chain nose pliers

♦ Scissors

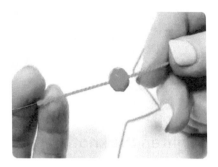

1 As tightly as possible, tie a knot about ½" away from the bottom of the silk cord (the opposite end from the needle). Slide the first bead onto the cord until it reaches and sits above the knot.

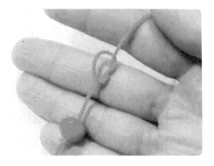

2 Tie a loose knot close to the first bead.

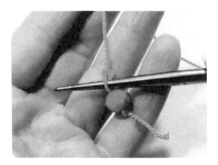

3 Using the awl, slide the knot (see here) so it is just over the bead.

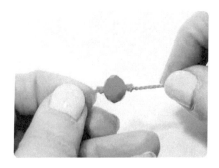

4 Remove the awl and tighten the knot.

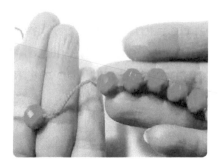

5 Slide another bead onto the cord and use the awl to knot. Repeat until you have knotted 16 beads onto the cord. At this point, wrap the cord around your wrist and check to see if the first and last bead (almost) meet on the inside of your wrist. If they do, you can stop and move on to step 6. If you need to lengthen the bracelet, add an additional bead and check again. Repeat as many times as necessary.

6 Cut the cord about ½" above the last bead. This will separate the attached needle from your beaded cord.

7 **(pictured above)** Hold the end of an open clamshell connector with a pair of chain nose pliers. Using a scrap piece of wire or toothpick, dab a small dot of glue on the inside of one side of the clamshell.

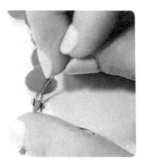

8 Place one side of the end knot into the clamshell and press it down into the glue. Dab another dot of glue on the top of the knot.

9 Using the chain nose pliers, lightly but firmly close the clamshell over the knot.

10 Holding the tail that is left below the closed clamshell, cut it with scissors as close to the clamshell as possible. If you need to, you can trim away any stray fibers that are there afterward.

11 Using two pliers open and attach the 8mm jump ring (see here) and the lobster clasp to one clamshell end of the bracelet. Open and attach the 12mm jump ring to the other end.

> **TIP:** *The cord needs to fit tightly around your wrist because adding the jump rings and closure will make the bracelet longer. This is why the first and last bead should "almost" but not quite meet on the inside of your wrist.*

> **TIP:** *For an interesting look, use an assortment of bead colors or create an ombre effect.*

You can try all kinds of fabulous color combinations for these fun fringe earrings. Feel free to use different colors of metal wire and jump rings to change up the look.

TECHNIQUES LEARNED

◆ Working with seed beads

◆ Making fish hook earring wires with head pins

◆ Making an earring base with wire

MATERIALS

◆ Seed beads

◆ 248 of color A (blue)

◆ 234 of color B (fuchsia)

◆ 180 of color C (orange)

◆ 144 of color D (pink)

◆ 18 pieces of 9" Nymo size D beading thread

◆ 2 (2") head pins or fish hook earring wires

◆ 2 (12mm) jump rings

◆ 2 (6") pieces of 22-gauge wire

TOOLS

◆ Round nose pliers

◆ Flush cutters

◆ Chain nose pliers

◆ Size 10 beading needle

◆ Small embroidery scissors

With the nose pliers, grip the wire and... the tip

MAKE THE EARRING BASE

1 Using the round nose pliers, make a small simple loop (see here) at one end of one of the pieces of 6" wire.

2 Measure about ¾" of the wire, including the looped area, and keep your finger on that spot of the wire.

3 With the chain nose pliers, bend the wire up at the measured spot.

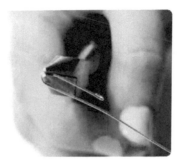

4 Bend the wire a little more so that it is folded in half.

5 Open the wire up a bit.

6 Make another bend aligned with the curved end of the wire.

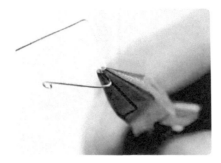

7 Use the chain nose pliers to define the bent corners more if necessary, so that they are sharp angles, forming a triangle base.

8 With the cutters, trim the end of the wire that does not have a loop, leaving enough wire so that you can make another loop with the round nose pliers, as in step 1.

9 Repeat step 1 on the straight wire end, making a small simple loop with the round nose pliers.

10 Using 2 pliers, open a jump ring (see <u>here</u>).

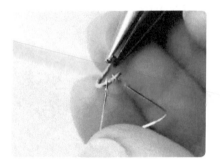

11 Attach the loops of the triangle-shaped earring base to the open jump ring.

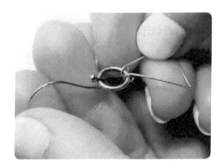

12 Attach the jump ring to a fish hook earring wire. You can either buy a premade finding or make your own (see <u>here</u>), using round nose pliers to curve a head pin around a mandrel or pen. Repeat steps 1 to 12 to make a second earring base.

MAKE THE FRINGE

1 Thread a needle with 9" of Nymo thread.

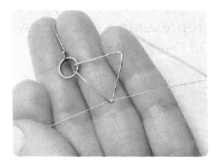

2 Tie the end of the thread to the triangle earring base with a knot, leaving about a 4" tail.

3 When stringing seed beads, lay out beads in a single layer and use the tip of your needle to pick them up, then push them onto the thread.

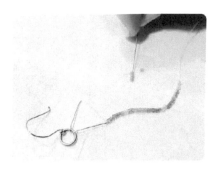

4 String the beads onto the thread, toward the triangle base, in the following pattern: 3A, 2B, 1C, 2D, 2A, 4C, 2B, 2A, 1B, 2D, 4B, 1C, 2A, 2D, 4C, 1D, 1B, 1A, 3B, 2A, 1D. Each number represents the number of beads and each letter represents a color. In my design A is blue, B is fuchsia, C is orange, and D is pink.

5 Skipping the bottom bead, bring the needle and thread up through all the beads you strung on.

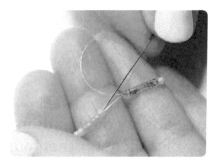

6 If your needle is not long enough to go through all the beads at once, you may take up a few beads at a time and pull the beads downward as you go, to make room for more beads.

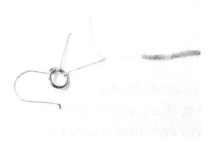

7 Tighten the beads by pushing them up on the thread (except for the bottom pink bead), toward the triangle base, and pulling the needle to take up the slack of thread that will occur below the beads.

8 Keep doing this until there is no gap between the thread at the triangle wire base and the beads are sitting beneath it. The bottom pink bead will have tightened up when the thread was pulled.

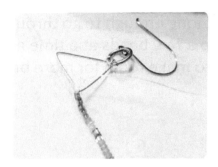

9 With the main thread and the tail thread on opposite sides of the triangle base, triple knot the two threads together around the base. For added strength, you can use a toothpick to place a dot of glue on the finished knots.

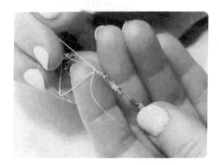

10 Using the needle, bring the main thread down through a number of beads.

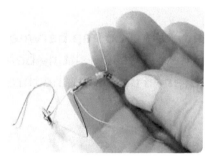

11 You will now have thread coming out partway down the first fringe.

12 Trim the thread with embroidery scissors, as close to the bead as possible.

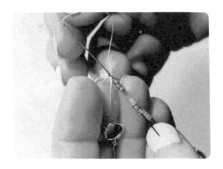

13 Trim the tail thread as well.

14 Repeat step 4 with a new piece of Nymo thread, using 4 A beads instead of 3. All the other beads on this thread will be exactly the same quantity. Do this 2 more times, each time tying a new piece of thread on the wire base and adding one more bead at the top. You will have a total of five beaded threads, the first starting with 3 A beads at the top, the second starting with 4 A beads, the third starting with 5 A beads, the fourth starting with 6 A beads, and the fifth starting with 7 A beads.

15 Make four more beaded threads, this time going lower in bead quantity, by one bead each time: the sixth thread starting with 6 A beads at the top, the seventh with 5 A beads, the eighth with 4 A beads, and the ninth with 3 A beads. Repeat all the steps to make a second earring.

PINK LOTUS NECKLACE

There is something magical about the way the three strands of this necklace fall into place when worn. This project is a bit time-consuming due to the number of beads used, but well worth it for the gorgeous result.

TECHNIQUES LEARNED

♦ Making a head pin charm

♦ Working with chain

♦ Stringing multiple bead strands

MATERIALS

For Head Pin Charm

♦ 1 (2") head pin

♦ 2 (6mm) disk spacer beads

♦ 2 (3mm) seed beads

♦ 1 lotus focal bead

For Necklace

♦ 253 (3mm) TOHO seed beads

♦ 8 (6mm) faceted fire-polished beads

♦ 4 (6mm) faceted fire-polished beads (in a different color from the 8 (6mm) beads)

♦ 276 size 11 Czech seed beads

♦ 2 (12mm) jump rings

♦ 2 pieces of 2 ¼" length chain

♦ 4 (4.5mm) jump rings

- 1 (12mm) lobster clasp
- 6 (2mm) crimp tubes
- 3 pieces of nylon-coated stainless steel jewelry wire in these sizes: 14",17", 19"

TOOLS
- Flush cutters
- Round nose pliers
- 2 pairs of chain nose pliers
- Crimping pliers

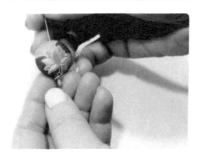

MAKE THE HEAD PIN CHARM

1 Slide 1 of the seed beads onto the head pin. Follow with a disk spacer bead and then the focal bead. Next, add another disk spacer bead and top off with a seed bead.

2 Using flush cutters, cut the head pin about ⅜ " above the top bead.

3 With the round nose pliers, make a simple loop above the beads (see here).

MAKE THE BEADED NECKLACE STRANDS

1 Using the crimping pliers, attach a crimp tube (see here) to a 14" piece of jewelry wire, creating a loop at the end of the jewelry wire. (Alternately, you can attach a bead stopper about 1" from the wire end.)

2 String beads on in the following pattern: 2 TOHO seed beads, 6 Czech seed beads. Repeat this 21 more times and then end with 2 TOHO seed beads.

3 Repeat step 1 with the 17" piece of jewelry wire. Then string on only the TOHO seed beads (147 of them).

4 Repeat step1 again with the 19" piece of jewelry wire and the following patterns: 2 TOHO seed beads, 6 Czech seed beads. Repeat this 8 more times and end with 2 TOHO seed beads. 1 fire-polished bead, 1 alternate color fire-polished bead, 1 fire-polished bead (same as the first color), 2 TOHO seed beads, 6 Czech seed beads. Repeat this 1 more time and end with 2 TOHO beads. 1 fire-polished bead, 1 alternate color fire-polished bead, 1 fire-polished bead (same as the first color), 2 TOHO seed beads, 6 Czech seed beads. 2 TOHO seed beads, bead charm.

5 After the bead charm, string on a mirror image of the beads placed on the other side.

6 Using the crimping pliers, attach a crimp tube (see here), creating a loop at the end of the three jewelry wires. Repeat this process on the other end of the wires if you used a bead stopper and did not do it at the beginning. Be sure to trim any excess wire if necessary.

7 Attach the end of each bead strand to an open 12mm jump ring (see here), making sure the shortest strand is closest to the top, followed by the middle-size strand, then the longest strand.

8 Close the jump ring. Repeat on the other side with the second 12mm jump ring.

9 Open and attach the 4.5mm jump ring and 2¼" length of chain to the 12mm jump ring on one side of the necklace.

10 Open and attach another 4.5mm jump ring and 2¼" piece of chain to the 12mm jump ring on the other side of the necklace.

11 Open and attach a 4.5mm jump ring and the lobster clasp to the right end of the necklace. Open and attach the other 4.5mm jump ring to the left end.

TIP: *There are many beads in this project and most of them are very small. In order to stay organized, you may want to use a bead board to lay out the design because the beads don't slip around and the shape allows you to envision what it will look like as a finished jewelry piece. You can also lay them down on a towel.*

DAPPLED LIGHT
NECKLACE

RADIANT IN
RED EARRINGS

I'M CHARMED
BRACELET

129

CHAPTER 5

∾ WIRE ∾
WRAPPING

This chapter features projects that will let you use the wire-working skills you learned earlier in the book, as well as introduce some new ones. These exciting projects include the easy-to-make and adaptable Hibiscus Flower Drop Earrings and Dappled Light Necklace, which will allow you to practice your bead wrapping skills. There is a range of simple to more complex projects so that you can get started right away, even if you have no wire-working experience at all.

DON'T BE BLUE BRACELET

HIBISCUS FLOWER DROP EARRINGS

Don't feel like you need to use the same exact beads I use in a design. Let your creativity shine by experimenting with bead colors and shapes. Make several pairs of these earrings to wear with different outfits or give as gifts to your friends. Use the sizes listed here as a guide (6mm round and 12mm shaped beads) and try any type of bead you like, from pearls to hearts and stars. You'll be amazed by how many fun looks you can achieve with such a simple design!

TECHNIQUES LEARNED

◆ Making earring wires with head pins
◆ Working with head pins

MATERIALS

◆ 2 (3mm) faceted rondelle beads
◆ 2 (6mm) round Czech glass beads
◆ 2 (12mm) flat flower-shaped glass beads, identical on both sides
◆ 4 (2") brass color ball head pins

TOOLS

◆ Flush cutters
◆ Round nose pliers
◆ Mandrel (optional)

1 Slide 1 (3mm) faceted rondelle bead onto a ball head pin, add 1 (6mm) round bead, and 1 (12mm) flower-shaped bead to finish the design.

2 Using the flush cutters, cut off most of the wire, leaving about ⅜ " above the top bead. When cutting your second beaded head pin, you can hold the first one next to it in order to eyeball your cut mark and ensure each pin is the same length.

3 With the pliers, grasp the wire, just above the beads, and bend it at a right angle.

4 Grasp the end of the wire with the round nose pliers. With a rotating motion, curve the wire around the top jaw, in the opposite direction, until it creates a simple loop (see here). Use the middle of the round nose pliers, which results in a slightly larger loop. Straighten the curve so that it aligns with the pin.

5 Make a set of fish hook earring wires using round nose pliers to curve the head pin around a mandrel or pen, or use store-bought earring wires.

6 Slide the loop of the beaded head pin onto the earring wire until it is attached to the loop of the earring wire. Repeat all steps for the second earring.

TIP: *As you are cutting the head pin, place your hand lightly over the cutters to catch the cut piece of the head pin and prevent it from flying out and possibly injuring you.*

MARKETPLACE CHANDELIER EARRINGS

DIFFICULTY RATING: 2 • START TO FINISH TIME: 20 MINUTES

These earrings are another quick but lovely project—perfect for beginners. Once you have learned the techniques, try adding multiple looped beads for a longer earring with even more movement.

TECHNIQUES LEARNED

- Making earring wires with head pins
- Working with jump rings
- Making an earring dangle with a head pin

MATERIALS

- 2 chandelier earring findings
- 14 (2") head pins
- 12 (4.5mm) jump rings
- 12 (2mm) beads
- 2 (8mm) beads
- 2 Czech glass disk spacer beads

TOOLS

- Flush cutters
- Round nose pliers
- 2 pairs of chain nose pliers

1 Thread a disk spacer bead onto a ball head pin, followed by an 8mm bead, and then a 2mm bead.

2 Using the flush cutters, cut the head pin about ⅜" above the top bead.

3 Using the round nose pliers, rotate the wire around the pliers' jaw, to create a simple loop above the beads (see <u>here</u>).

4 Using 2 pliers, open a jump ring (see <u>here</u>) and attach it to the looped beads.

5 Using the jump ring, attach the looped beads to the bridge at the top of the chandelier finding. Repeat steps 1 to 5 for the second earring.

6 Repeat steps 1 to 3, using only 1 (2mm) bead.

7 Do this 10 times, so that you have a total of 10 looped 2mm beads.

8 Using 2 pliers, open 10 jump rings and attach each looped 2mm bead onto the rings at the bottom of the chandelier findings.

9 Make a set of fish hook earring wires using round nose pliers to curve the 2 head pins around a mandrel or pen, or use store-bought earring wires. Attach the earring wires to the chandelier finding.

TIP: *Some people have allergies to metal. If this is an issue for you or your gift recipient, try using niobium or surgical steel wire when making your earring wires. It is also possible to purchase hypoallergenic metal earring wires that are premade.*

WRAPPED BRIOLETTE PENDANT

DIFFICULTY RATING: 2 • START TO FINISH TIME: 20 MINUTES

Wrapping briolette beads transforms them into adaptable charms that you can use as a bracelet decoration or necklace pendant, or for earrings. There are many beautiful crystal products available in the marketplace. Swarovski is the most popular brand of crystal beads but also one of the most expensive. You may choose to go with Swarovski due to the assured quality behind the name, or explore other crystal products available, some of which are equal in quality.

TECHNIQUES LEARNED

◆ Wire wrapping
◆ Making a pendant with wire

MATERIALS

◆ 12" (22-gauge) jewelry wire
◆ 1 top-drilled briolette bead

TOOLS

◆ Chain nose pliers
◆ Nylon jaw pliers
◆ Round nose pliers
◆ Flush cutters

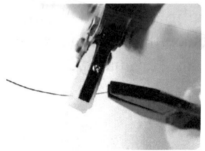

1 Holding one end of the wire with the chain nose pliers, use the nylon jaw pliers to straighten out any bends in the wire.

2 Thread the briolette bead onto the wire, leaving about ¾" on one side.

3 Bend both sides of the wire in an upward motion.

4 Using the round nose pliers, squeeze the base of the wire sides together above the briolette bead.

5 Bring the longer wire closer to you.

6 Use the round nose pliers to create a curve in the long wire, by wrapping it around the bottom pliers toward you.

7 Reposition the round nose pliers so that one pliers' jaw is inside the loop and the other is outside the loop, then finish making a circle, by wrapping the rest of the wire around the pliers' jaw.

8 Hold the short wire tail and the circle you just made firmly with the chain nose pliers.

9 Wrap the long wire tail around the shorter wire in a downward motion until you have reached the opening of the bead.

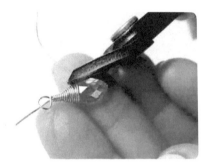

10 With the flush cutters, trim the short tail and the long tail if there is any wire left.

11 Use the chain nose pliers to gently squeeze the sharp point of wire down next to the wrap.

TIP: *If you would like to be able to thread your briolette wrap on a chain, use the wider part of the round nose pliers when making the loop. For a smaller loop, use the smaller part. You can use a jump ring to attach a smaller looped briolette pendant on a chain.*

DON'T BE BLUE BRACELET

The decorative bar portion of this project comes together easily. Add just a couple pieces of chain and connecting components to it and, voilà, you have a pretty bracelet.

TECHNIQUES LEARNED

◆ Working with eye pins

◆ Working with chain

◆ Attaching chain with clamshell crimps

MATERIALS

◆ 2 pieces of chain 1.5" or longer, depending on wrist size (use a tape measure to measure your wrist; subtract 2½" from the wrist measurement. Cut 2 pieces of chain that equal the length of this number.)

◆ 4 (5mm or slightly larger) jump rings

◆ 1 (11mm or slightly larger) lobster clasp

◆ 1 (2") eye pin

◆ 2 (2mm) round beads

◆ 2 (4mm) round beads

◆ 2 (6mm) faceted beads

◆ 1 (12mm) coin-shaped bead

◆ 4 (7.3 × 3.7 × 3.3mm, or slightly larger) clamshell crimp connectors

◆ Glue (Power Grab by Loctite is a good brand)

TOOLS

- ♦ **2 pairs of chain nose pliers**
- ♦ **Round nose pliers**
- ♦ **Flush cutters**

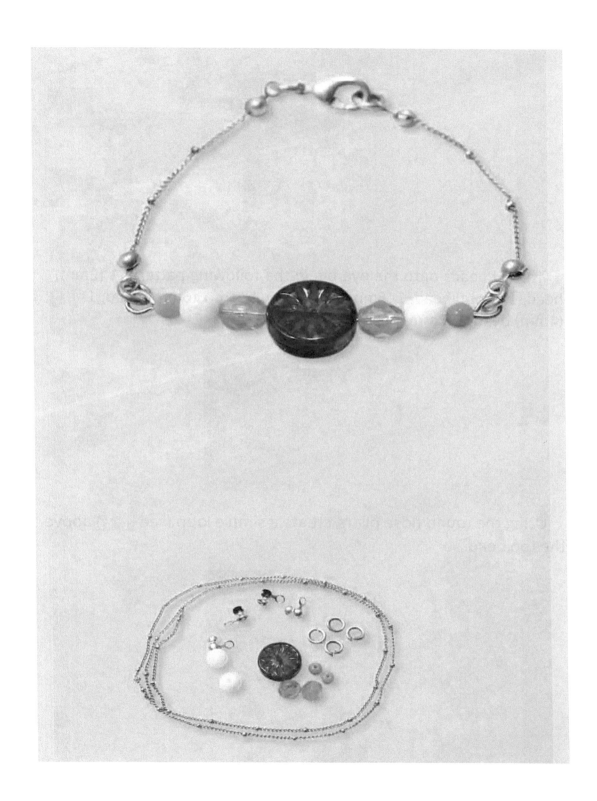

1 Thread beads onto the eye pin in the following pattern: 1 (2mm) bead, 1 (4mm) bead, 1 (6mm) bead, coin bead, 1 (6mm) bead, 1 (4mm) bead, 1 (2mm) bead.

2 Using the round nose pliers, create a simple loop (see here) above the top bead.

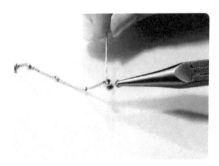

3 Attach the clamshell crimps (see <u>here</u>) to the 2 pieces of chain with glue.

4 Using chain nose pliers, lightly but firmly close the clamshell over the chain. Attach the 4 clamshell crimps to both ends of each piece of chain.

5 Open and attach a jump ring (see <u>here</u>) to connect the chain that you attached with the clamshell crimp loop to the loop on the beaded eye pin. Repeat on the other side of the beaded eye pin.

6 Open and attach a jump ring and lobster clasp to the clamshell crimp loop at the bracelet end. Open and attach a jump ring to the clamshell crimp loop at the other bracelet end.

TIP: *You can make all kinds of design variations with this project. Just add a longer chain to make a necklace. You could even include a hanging charm or charms using jump rings on the beaded bar.*

I'M CHARMED BRACELET

Charm bracelets are a fun way to create a personalized piece of jewelry, especially when giving one as a gift. Consider charms with initials, favorite colors, or birthstone beads.

TECHNIQUES LEARNED

◆ Wire wrapping with beads

◆ Wire coiling

◆ Working with memory wire

MATERIALS

◆ 2 (3mm) beads

◆ 2 charms of choice

◆ 1 (10mm) round bead

◆ 1 flower-shaped bead (or other shape of choice)

◆ 5 (2") head pins

◆ 2 (11") pieces of 24-gauge wire

◆ 2 (3") pieces of 24-gauge wire

◆ bracelet-sized memory wire

◆ 3 small segments of chain varying slightly in length, the first being ¾" long, the second slightly shorter, and the third slightly shorter than the second.

◆ 5 (5.4mm) jump rings

◆ 4 (4.5mm) jump rings

TOOLS

- ◆ Memory wire cutters
- ◆ Round nose pliers
- ◆ Chain nose pliers
- ◆ Nylon jaw pliers

155

MAKE THE BRACELET BASE

1 Wrap the memory wire around your wrist—it should not be too loose. Using your memory wire cutters (see Tip), cut one loop of bracelet-sized memory wire with about 1" of overlap.

2 Using the round nose pliers, make a small loop at one end of the wire. Face the loop so that when the bracelet is worn, the loop will sit parallel against the wearer's wrist. Use the chain nose pliers to move the loop. It may take a few tries because the wire is strong.

3 Coil one of the 11" pieces of 24-gauge wire around the memory bracelet starting at the base of the end loop. If necessary, use the chain nose pliers to pinch the beginning wraps around the memory wire lightly and then to twist 2 or 3 coils around the base.

4 You may have small gaps between some of the first few coils. If so, use the chain nose pliers to gently press the coils close together.

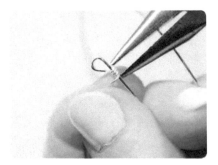

5 After pressing the coils together with the chain nose pliers they should look like this.

6 After you have a few starter loops secured, continue to wrap the 24-gauge wire by hand tightly in a clockwise motion until you have used all of it. Use the nylon jaw pliers to hold the finished coils in place as you add new coils.

7 Smooth out the coiling wire with your fingers as you're working, to prevent kinks.

8 Once you have finished coiling the first 11" piece of 24-gauge wire around the memory wire, slide a 3mm bead onto the memory wire.

9 Slide the 3mm bead on the left side over until it meets the end of the coiled wire. Coil one of the 3" pieces of 24-gauge wire next to the bead so that the bead is sandwiched between the larger coils and this second segment of coil.

10 As you are working, gently squeeze the coils against the memory wire with the chain nose pliers, so that they don'lt slide around, holding the 3mm bead in place.

11 String on the charms (instructions for making charms follow).

12 Slide the other 3mm bead onto the wire.

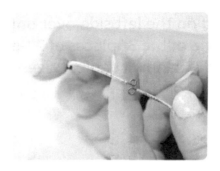

13 Repeat steps 2-7 on the other side of the bracelet. Create the same kind of loop you did in step 2, but facing the opposite direction so that when placed together the two loops look like a figure 8. Repeat steps 9-10 for the second bead.

MAKE THE CHARMS

1 Attach the 2 premade charms onto one 5.4mm jump ring each (see here).

2 Make a looped wrap with the 10mm bead, using a head pin (see here).

3 Repeat step 2 for the flower-shaped bead.

4 Take the 3 (3mm) beads and form simple loops with each of them using the simple loop technique (see here).

5 Using three 4.5mm jump rings, attach the 3 looped beads onto the ends of the chains.

6 Using another 4.5mm jump ring, attach the tops of the 3 segments of chain to it and attach this piece to the bracelet using a 5.4mm jump ring.

7 Attach all the other charms as desired to the bracelet, using a 5.4mm jump ring for each.

TIP: *Be sure not to use your regular flush cutters to cut memory wire, as it is harder than other jewelry wire and will mar your cutters. You can use special memory wire cutters or a pair of sturdy flush cutters that you keep aside for using only on memory wire.*

DROPS OF SUMMER HOOP EARRINGS

DIFFICULTY RATING: 2 • START TO FINISH TIME: 1 HOUR

With just a bit of wire and a few simple tools, you can make the prettiest go-with-everything hoop earrings.

TECHNIQUES LEARNED

◆ Manipulating wire

◆ Hammering wire

◆ Straightening wire

◆ Making a wrapped loop bead charm

MATERIALS

◆ 2 (2") head pins

◆ 2 beads of choice

◆ 2 (4") pieces of 20-gauge jewelry wire

TOOLS

◆ Nylon jaw pliers

◆ Round nose pliers

◆ Flush cutters

◆ Chain nose pliers

◆ Mallet or chasing hammer

◆ Steel bench block

◆ Emery board

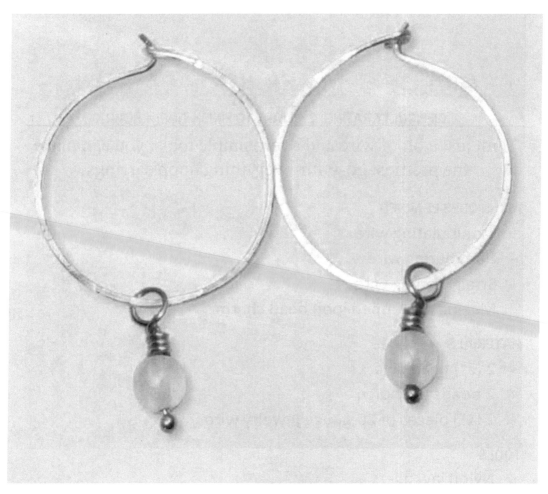

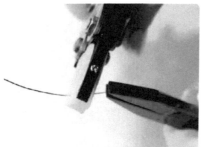

1 Use nylon jaw pliers to straighten out a length of the jewelry wire, about 4" long. Work with wire attached to the spool since the length you will need depends on the size of the object you'll wrap it around in step 2.

2 Choose a cylindrical object and wrap the wire around it, leaving an overlap of 1" or so of extra wire. You could use a ring mandrel or a household object. I am using a small bead container for a larger size hoop.

3 Using the chain nose pliers, make a curved open loop at the end of your wire.

4 With the flush cutters, cut the wire about ¾" longer than where it comes around the loop to make a full circle.

5 Use round nose pliers to create a bend at the end of the wire.

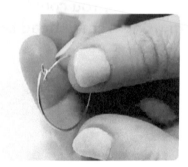

6 The wire end will fit into the curved loop to close the earring. Trim this end to your preferred length.

7 Use an emery board to file down the sharp wire end. Wrap wire around the cylindrical object again to correct any bends or kinks in

the hoop.

8 Place the hoop on a bench block and lightly hammer all around the wire, except for the top area where the closure is. You will want to keep this rounded for the proper fit when wearing the earrings. Repeat hammering 2 or 3 more times. This will harden the wire a bit, giving it more springiness and preventing it from easily losing shape. Test the hoop to make sure that you've hammered enough by gently pulling the two sides of the hoop apart. If the shape springs back, you are finished hammering. If the hoop loses its shape, shape it around the cylindrical object again and hammer a bit more.

9 Slide a bead onto a head pin and make a wrapped loop bead (see here). Slide the bead onto the earring. Repeat all the steps to make a second earring.

TIP: *If you prefer to keep the rounded shape of the wire rather than flattening it out, use a rubber or rawhide mallet, instead of metal.*

Experiment with different types of bead charms; you can even mix and match with this jewelry staple for many fun looks!

SUNSHINE SPIRAL EARRINGS

DIFFICULTY RATING: 3 • START TO FINISH TIME: 30 MINUTES

These whimsical earrings teach you to create a spiral, a technique that can also be applied to necklace charms as well as head pins.

TECHNIQUES LEARNED

◆ Wire bead wrapping

◆ Making fish hook earring wires

◆ Working with wire

MATERIALS

◆ 2 (9") pieces of 20-gauge wire

◆ 2 (6mm) beads

◆ 2 (4mm) beads

◆ 2 (2") head pins or fish hook earring wires

TOOLS

◆ Round nose pliers

◆ Nylon jaw pliers

◆ Flush cutters

1 With the round nose pliers, grasp the end of the wire and rotate the pliers to make a curve. Continue until you make a medium-size loop. Position the wire toward the center of the pliers' jaws to get a medium-size loop.

2 Hold the loop firmly, but not too tightly, with the nylon jaw pliers. With your fingers, wrap the wire in a spiraling motion around the center loop until you have 5 coils making up a spiral shape.

3 Bend the wire above the spiral into a 90-degree angle.

4 Thread the 6mm bead onto the wire, then the 4mm bead.

5 Make a wrapped loop above the bead (see here). Align the loop with the spiral so that the front of the earring will be visible when worn on its earring wire.

6 Trim off the excess wire with the flush cutters.

7 Make a <u>fish hook earring wire</u> using round nose pliers to curve a head pin around a mandrel or pen, or use a store-bought earring wire. Attach your spiral to the earring wire. Repeat all of the steps to make the second earring.

> TIP: *You can make your spirals as small or as large as you wish. Experiment with various beads and sizes for unique looks.*

CAGED BEAD

You can experiment and use a variety of bead shapes and sizes. Adjust the length of wire so it is shorter if using a smaller bead, or longer if using a larger bead. Caged beads can be linked together to make bracelets or kept as is for a pendant. There are many ways to incorporate this versatile finding into your jewelry creations.

TECHNIQUES LEARNED

◆ Making spirals with wire

◆ Making your own bead

MATERIALS

◆ 1 (8") piece of 18-or 20-gauge wire

◆ 1 (3") piece of 18-or 20-gauge wire

◆ 1 (10mm) round bead

TOOLS

◆ Flat nose pliers

◆ Nylon jaw pliers

◆ Round nose pliers

◆ Flush cutters

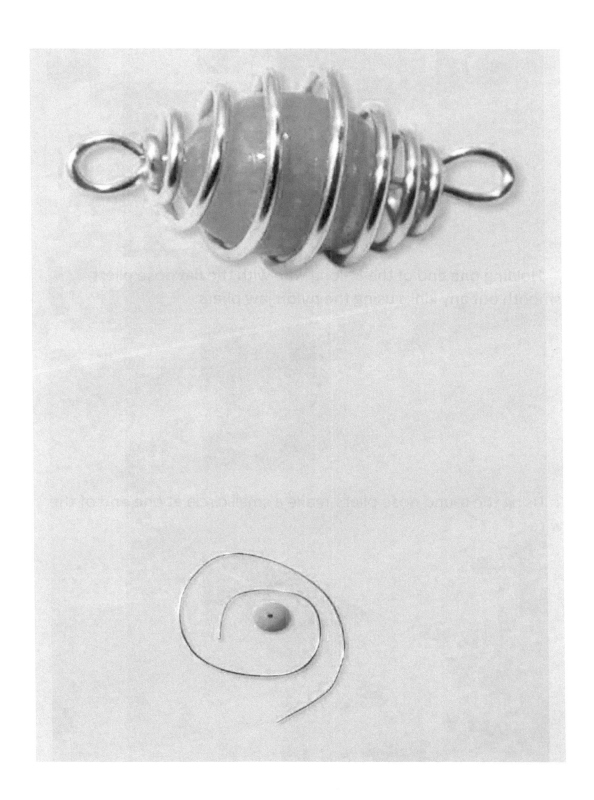

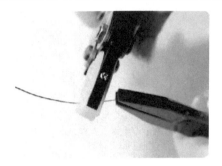

1 Holding one end of the 8"-long wire with the flat nose pliers, smooth out any kinks using the nylon jaw pliers.

2 Using the round nose pliers, make a small circle at one end of the wire.

3 Hold the circle tightly in the nylon jaw pliers and rotate it around in a clockwise motion, adding more wire to create a spiral.

4 On the other side of the spiral repeat step 2, making a small circle, facing the opposite direction of the first circle.

5 Begin making a spiral on this side as well and go back and forth between the two sides, adding to the spirals until they meet in the middle.

6 In the same direction for both, place the round nose pliers into the center hole of each spiral and push up, while gently pulling down on each coil, so the spirals take on a conical shape.

7 This is what the conical shape should look like.

8 Bend the spirals in half so the wide parts are facing each other.

9 Open the wire bead so that you can fit the round bead inside.

10 Using your fingers, squeeze the wire bead down around the round bead so it completely encloses it.

11 Thread the 3"-long wire through the end holes in the wire bead and the round bead, so that the long wire comes through the other side.

12 Make an <u>eye pin</u> with the 3"-long wire.

13 Cut the eye pin about ⅜ " above the wire bead and, as in step 12, also make a loop on this end.

14 Adjust the wire bead loops so that they are even and to your liking.

TIP: *Take extra care to make sure the 3"-long wire is properly aligned when placing it through the wire wrapping and the bead, so that it doesn't end up entering or exiting through the wrong part of the wire wrapping or "spiral."*

TIP: *The nylon jaw pliers are used to prevent scratching the surface of the wire, which has a lot of contact with pliers in this project. Chain nose pliers could be used instead, but be extra careful to prevent marring the wire.*

DAPPLED LIGHT NECKLACE

This project provides lots of opportunity for practicing your wrapping technique. If you prefer, you can easily make this dainty necklace into a statement piece by using larger beads.

TECHNIQUES LEARNED

◆ Wire bead wrapping

◆ Wire briolette bead wrapping

◆ Working with chain

◆ Making a hammered wire S-hook clasp

MATERIALS

◆ 1 (17") piece of necklace chain

◆ 9 (4.5mm) jump rings

◆ 6 (6mm) round beads

◆ 1 (13mm) briolette bead

◆ 1 (10") piece of 22-gauge wire

◆ 6 (2") head pins

◆ 1 S-hook hammered wire clasp (make your own, see here)

TOOLS

◆ Round nose pliers

◆ Flush cutters

◆ Chain nose pliers

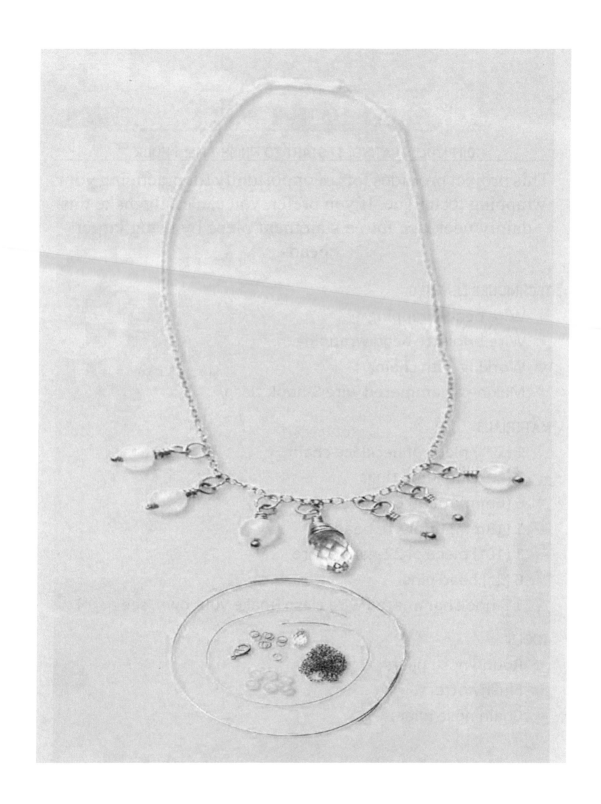

182

1 Wrap the briolette with wire as explained in the <u>Wrapped Briolette Pendant</u> project.

2 Wrap a round bead with wire (see <u>here</u>). Repeat 5 more times.

3 Fold the necklace chain in half to find the center link and attach the wrapped briolette here with a jump ring (see <u>here</u>).

4 Count 5 chain links over from the center and attach the wrapped round bead to the fifth chain link. Repeat 2 more times on this side and then do the same 3 times on the other side.

5 Open and attach a jump ring to the left side of the necklace; attach another jump ring on the other side. Attach the S hook clasp to the jump rings.

CITRUS ON YOUR WRIST BRACELET

Though this project utilizes just one technique, the result is sophisticated and complex looking. You can simplify this bracelet if you like by creating simple loops instead of wrapped loops.

TECHNIQUES LEARNED

♦ Making wrapped bead connectors
♦ Connecting wrapped bead segments with jump rings

MATERIALS

♦ 7 or 8 pieces of 2½" 20-gauge wire
♦ 8 or 9 (4.5mm) jump rings
♦ 4 (6mm) beads
♦ 3 or 4 (3mm) seed beads
♦ 6 or 8 (3mm) beads of choice
♦ 1 loop and toggle clasp

TOOLS

♦ Flat nose pliers
♦ Nylon jaw pliers
♦ Flush cutters
♦ Round nose pliers
♦ 2 pairs of chain nose pliers

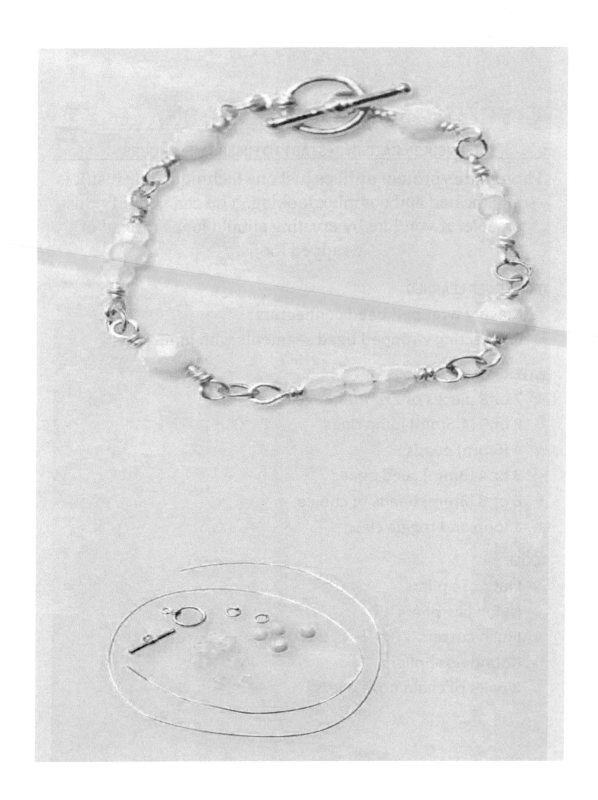

186

Make a wrapped loop at the other end of the wire, add another bead.

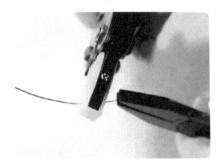

1 Hold the end of one of the wire pieces with the flat nose pliers and use the nylon jaw pliers to smooth out any kinks.

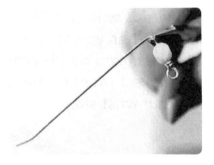

2 Slide 1 of the 6mm beads onto the wire and make a wrapped loop at one end (here).

3 Make a wrapped loop at the other side of the bead, so that there is a loop on both ends. Trim off excess wire with flush cutters.

4 Repeat steps 2 and 3, this time with three beads in this pattern: 3mm bead, seed bead, 3mm bead.

5 Make a total of 4 bead wraps with the 6mm beads and 3 bead wraps with the 3mm beads. When you are near the completion of the project, you will place the linked beads around your wrist to determine if you need to make 1 more of the wrapped 3mm bead segments, depending on your wrist size.

6 Link the wrapped bead segments together using jump rings (see here), alternating between 6mm bead and 3mm bead segments.

7 Continue linking until you have linked all the segments together. Then, place the chain of beads onto your wrist and note how much space is between the ends. If there is just enough space for your toggle clasp to fit, you are good to go! If there is more space than the size of the toggle clasp, make 1 more wrapped bead segment and add it to the chain.

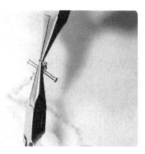

8 Attach the loop and toggle clasp pieces to the chain ends using jump rings.

TIP: *You can make this bracelet using simple looped beads if you prefer, or even mix and match with both looped beads and wrapped loop beads.*

RADIANT IN RED EARRINGS

DIFFICULTY RATING: 3 • START TO FINISH TIME: 2 HOURS

This elegant earring design is achieved with basic wire and beads.

TECHNIQUES LEARNED

- Wire wrapping with beads
- Making earring wires with head pins

MATERIALS

- 44 (4mm) TOHO cube seed beads
- 2 (51.5 x 18mm) teardrop-shaped wire hoops (can use smaller shape/fewer beads)
- 2 (15") pieces of 24-gauge wire
- 2 (2") head pins or fish hook earring wires

TOOLS

- Flush cutters
- 2 chain nose pliers
- Round nose pliers

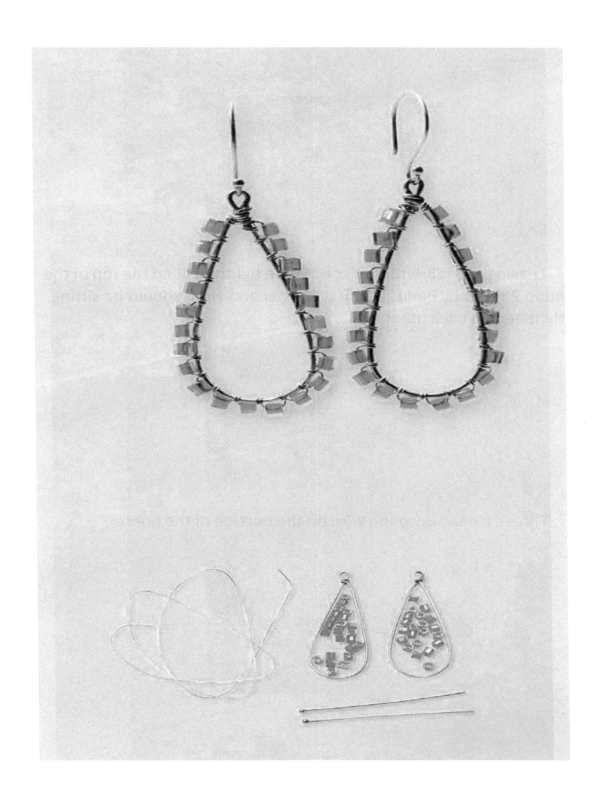

191

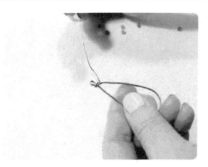

1 Leaving a 1" tail, wrap a piece of wire tightly around the top of the hoop 2 times by hand. The first and second wrap should be sitting right next to each other.

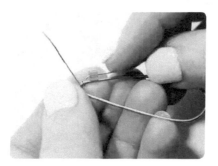

2 Thread a bead onto the wire on the outside of the hoop.

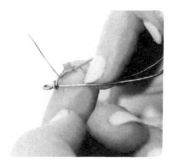

3 Holding the bead tightly next to the base of the first two wire wraps, secure it by wrapping the wire around the hoop 2 more times. This is your first wrapped bead. As you are wrapping the beads, use a pair of chain nose pliers to align them, making sure each bead sits at the outside of the hoop. You will be able to give the beads a final straightening at the end, after you've finished wrapping.

4 Repeat step 3 until you have wrapped all the beads around the hoop.

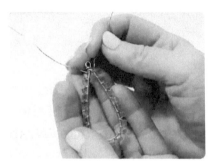

5 You should have about 1" left at the other end of your wire. If it is longer, trim with the flush cutters, leaving about a 1" tail.

6 Wrap this wire tail around your hoop end 3 or 4 times. Trim any wire that is left from this piece, placing it toward the inside of the hoop. Flatten the sharp wire end with chain nose pliers to eliminate any sharp edge.

7 With a pair of chain nose pliers, bring the other wire end (that you began the project with) over to the side of the finished wire and pull it through and tuck it under the end loop. Wrap the wire around 2 or 3 times. Pull taut and tight with the pliers.

8 Trim the excess wire and flatten the end with the chain nose pliers to eliminate any sharp edge. Repeat all the steps to create the second hoop earring.

9 Make 2 <u>fish hook earring wires</u> using round nose pliers to curve head pins around a mandrel or pen, or use store-bought earring wires. Attach the earring wires to the earrings.

TIP: *After you have wrapped all of your beads on the hoops, you can use a pair of chain nose pliers to straighten out any beads that have angled away from the outside of the hoops (these can shift out of place, even though you straightened your beads as you worked).*

SEASHELL COLLECTOR WRAP BRACELET

DIFFICULTY RATING: 2 • START TO FINISH TIME: 1.5 HOURS

Although it looks complicated, this memory wire wrap bracelet is super easy to make. Change up the beads and charms for a totally different look. For example, substitute purple beads for the blue ones in this project and swap crystal charms and tassels for seashells as in the design on the cover of this book.

TECHNIQUES LEARNED

♦ Working with memory wire
♦ Making jump ring charms

MATERIALS

♦ Bracelet-sized memory wire
♦ 40 (6mm) flower-shaped spacer beads
♦ 5 (14mm) flower-shaped Czech glass beads (or other decorative bead of choice)
♦ 24 (6mm) flat-disk Czech glass spacer beads
♦ 36 (4mm) TOHO cube glass beads
♦ 91 (1.5mm) TOHO cube seed beads
♦ 14 (6mm) flat metal spacer beads
♦ 42 (4mm) round seed beads
♦ 21 (6mm) faceted metal beads
♦ 13 (4mm) faceted metal beads

- 7 (6mm) melon-shaped Czech glass beads (or other style of choice)
- 2 assorted metal shell design beads (or other designs of choice)
- 2 (5mm, or larger) jump rings

TOOLS
- Round nose pliers
- Chain nose pliers
- Memory wire cutters

1 Using your memory wire cutters (see Tip_), cut the memory wire so that you are left with 5 coils of wire with about 1" of overlap. Using the round nose pliers, grasp the end of the memory wire; create a loop.

2 The loop should look like this.

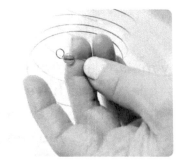

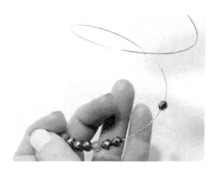

3 Thread beads onto the bracelet wire in the following patterns: 1 melon-shaped bead, 3 (6mm) faceted metal beads. Repeat 6 more times. 3 (4mm) round seed beads, 1 (6mm) flat metal spacer bead. Repeat 13 more times. 91 (1.5mm) TOHO cube seed beads. 3 (4mm) TOHO cube beads, 2 (6mm) flat Czech glass spacer beads. Repeat 11 more times. 5 (6mm) flower-shaped spacer beads, 1 (4mm) faceted metal bead, 1 (14mm) flower-shaped Czech bead, 1 (4mm) faceted metal bead, 5 (6mm) flower-shaped spacer beads, 1 (4mm) faceted metal bead. Repeat 2 times. 1 (14mm) Czech flower-shaped bead, 1 (4mm) faceted metal bead, 5 (6mm) flower-shaped spacer beads, 1 (4mm) faceted metal bead. Repeat 1 more time.

4 Close the bracelet by making another wire loop using round-nose pliers, as in step 1. This time, you will have a little bit of extra wire left.
5 Trim the excess wire at the inside of the loop, using memory wire cutters. If the wire sticks out a little, you can adjust the position of the wire end using chain nose pliers.

6 With a jump ring (see here), attach a shell charm to the beginning loop.

7 With another jump ring, attach a second shell charm to the end loop.

8 The finished bracelet is easy to put on and take off because the memory wire retains its shape.

TIP: *When stretched out, memory wire springs back into shape, similar to a Slinky toy. What can be tricky about working with this wire is that it occasionally gets tangled up. To avoid this, work slowly and hold the top portion of the wire as you slide beads on, letting gravity push the weight of the beads down and preventing the wire from curling up. If your wire does get tangled, be patient because it can take a little while to untangle. The more you use memory wire, the easier it will get.*

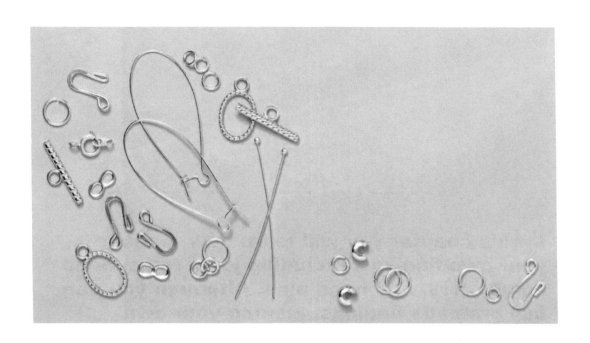

∽MAKE ∾

In this chapter you will learn how to make your own findings, including jump rings, bead connectors, and head pins. Although you can buy premade findings, making your own allows you to put your own unique style into the components you use in your jewelry making. This is also a great way to save money on supplies (and save your sanity if you happen to run out of something in the middle of a project).

You can use eye pins for a variety of projects, including linked bead bracelets, dangling charms, bar bracelets, and so much more.

Material **1 (3") piece of 20-or 22-gauge wire**

Tool **Round nose pliers**

1 Make a small loop at one end of the wire using the round nose pliers.

2 Turn the pliers slightly so that the loop is sitting straight above the long part of the wire.

Although jump rings are inexpensive to buy premade, it is helpful to know how to make your own in case you run out.

Material **1 (9½") piece of 20-or 22-gauge wire**

Tools **Mandrel or other small cylindrical object (such as a pen), flush cutters, emery board or file**

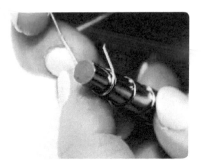

Coil the wire around a mandrel using the circumference that matches the size you need. You could use a pen instead if you prefer.

Add as many coils as you like. Each coil will make one jump ring.

Remove the coil from the mandrel. Stretch out the coiled wire a little.

Cut the wire, one loop at a time, until you have a little pile of jump rings.

With an emery board or file, smooth out the cut edges of each ring.

You can use DIY paddle head pins just as you'd use any other head pin—for example, to make a simple looped bead, a wrapped bead, or charms for necklaces or bracelets.

Material **1 (3") piece of 20-gauge wire**

Tools **Mallet or chasing hammer, bench block**

1 With your fingers, smooth out the wire a few times to straighten any kinks. This will also strengthen the wire a little bit.

2 Place ¼" or more of one end of the wire on the bench block. The length will depend on how much of the wire you would like to hammer into the decorative "paddle" portion of the head pin.

3 Using a mallet or chasing hammer, hammer the portion of the wire set on the bench block. Do this a few times, then turn the wire over and hammer the other side.

> **TIP:** *Test whether the head pin is finished by sliding a bead onto it. If the bead doesn't fall off, then the bottom or "paddle" portion of the head pin is ready.*

The ability to make head pin charms is an important foundational skill for any bead jewelry maker because they are so versatile. You can use head pin charms for bracelets, necklaces, and earrings, and to add a decorative touch to complement the look of a larger focal piece.

Materials **1 (2") head pin, 1 or more bead(s) of choice**
Tools **Flush cutters, round nose pliers**

Slide your bead or beads onto the head pin.

Using the flush cutters, cut the head pin about ⅜ " above the top bead.

With your fingers, push the top of the head pin down so it forms a right angle with the beaded portion.

Place the round nose pliers at the end of the head pin and turn until it meets the other side of the pin.

Adjust the loop slightly with the round nose pliers so that it is sitting straight on top of the beads below.

The spiral head pin adds a fun flair when you want something more than a simple head pin for an earring or charm project.

Material **1 (4") piece of 20-gauge wire**
Tools **Round nose pliers, nylon jaw pliers**

With your fingers, smooth out the wire to straighten out any kinks.

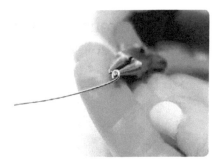

Make a small loop by rolling the end of the wire with the tip of the round nose pliers, until the end touches the straight part of the wire on the other side.

Hold the loop firmly but not too tightly with the nylon jaw pliers, and with your fingers, begin to wrap the wire in a spiraling motion around the center loop.

Continue to wrap the wire in a spiraling motion around the center loop until you have 3 coils making up a spiral shape.

Bend the base of the spiral slightly with the round nose pliers so that it is sitting straight above the long part of the wire.

TIP: *Nylon jaw pliers prevent the surface of metal wire from becoming scratched. They are useful for projects such as spiraling wire where the metal is coming into a lot of contact with the pliers.*

Making your own earring wires is quick. It will enable you to use a greater variety of metals and colors than store-bought earring wires.

Material **1 (2" or longer) ball head pin**
Tools **Round nose pliers, mandrel**

With round nose pliers, make a small looped curve at the ball end of the head pin.

Curve the head pin around the second or third segment of the mandrel.

Make a small curve at the non-ball end of the head pin. This will help keep the earrings from sliding off.

To make an earring using the earring wire, slide a charm on at the non-ball end of the wire and all the way through to the ball area. Push the charm past the ball; it will then be held in place.

Knowing how to make bead connectors is another invaluable skill to have in your arsenal as a bead jewelry maker. You can use them to link pieces of chain together, to make bracelets and necklaces, and also to connect clasps.

Materials **1 (2½") piece of 20-gauge wire, 1 or more bead(s) of choice**

Tools **Round nose pliers, 2 sets of chain nose pliers, flush cutters**

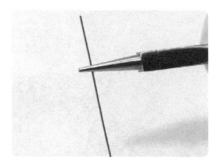

With flush cutters, cut a 2½" piece of wire. Hold the wire with round nose pliers ½" down from one end.

Bend the wire above the round nose pliers at a 90-degree angle. Then reposition the wire so that it is clamped in between the round nose pliers at the bend in the wire.

Grasp the wire with round nose pliers at the top of the bend and wrap the wire around the top jaw of the pliers, until it has formed a curve and the wire is pointing downward.

Reposition the round nose pliers so that the loop is on the opposite jaw, giving room to finish the circle. Push the wire until it has formed a circle.

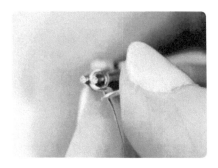

With the second set of chain nose pliers or your finger, wrap the wire end around the wire "neck" below the loop 2 times.

Slide bead(s) onto the wire.

Position round nose pliers ¼" above the last bead.

Repeat steps 2 to 4.

With the second set of chain nose pliers or your finger, wrap the wire end around the wire "neck" below the loop 2 times.

Trim off the excess wire with flush cutters. Use chain nose pliers to flatten the end of the wire against the loops.

TIP: *You can make bead connectors using the wrapped loop technique as described here or you can make them faster with simple loops.*

Wrapping the wire is good to strengthen a thinner 22-or 24-gauge wire. With a heavier wire, thicker than 20-gauge, it may be easier to do a simple loop. But if you prefer the wrapped loop look, go with it regardless of the wire gauge.

You can use this simple closure for bracelets and necklaces.

Material **1 (3") piece of 20-gauge wire**

Tools **Round nose pliers, mallet or chasing hammer, bench block**

With the largest part of the round nose pliers' jaw, make a curve about ½" away from the end of your wire.

Bend the end of the curved wire out slightly.

Make another large curve in the wire diagonally across from and identical in size to the curve you made in step 1.

Cut the wire below this second curve about ½" down.

Make a small bend at this end of the wire just like you did in step 2.

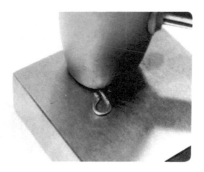

Hammer the S-hook on your bench block several times on one side. Turn the S-hook over and then hammer several times on the other side.

Check to see if your S-hook clasp is ready to use by gently bending one of the hooks out. If there is a lot of give and the hook easily loses its shape, it is not ready—it should be bent back into place by hand, then hammered some more. If there is not much give and the clasp feels strong, then it is ready.

TIP: *The size guidelines given in these directions are just a suggestion. You can adapt these instructions to any size you would like, depending on how large or small you need your clasp to be.*

PEACHY TASSEL
NECKLACE

225

⌒⊛SELL⊛⌒

It's easier than ever before to start your own business and sell your work. There can be very little cost and virtually no barrier to entry involved in getting started. Even with just one, two, or three killer items, a camera phone, and a few dollars' investment on an online selling platform like Etsy, you can be up and running in no time. Read on for some great tips on how you can start your own jewelry business.

PRACTICE MAKES PERFECT

Just like anything else, the more you practice making bead jewelry, the more skilled you will become and the better your pieces will look. Master a few techniques and make multiple projects with them. Eventually, all the repetition will pay off and you won't be able to tell the difference between your handcrafted items and those you'd find in a jewelry shop.

There are many jewelry artists selling their work, but one of the ways you can stand out is if your creations speak to your potential customer. For instance, design something that can be personalized, like a hand-stamped initial charm, or include a signature detail that is unique to your work. Consider what will attract buyers. Like your unique fingerprint, finding a personal style will help set your handmade work apart from anyone else's.

IT'S ALL IN THE MATERIALS

There is a seemingly endless sea of beads and materials available for you to choose. While it is perfectly reasonable to start out with less expensive supplies as you are learning, remember that the higher the quality of beads, findings, stringing materials, and tools you use, the better your jewelry is going to look. This is especially important if you are planning to eventually sell your work. For instance, spending more for beading jewelry wire instead of craft wire will make a big difference in the quality of your designs, adding value and making them more salable. If you are going to invest your time in something, it's worth it to use materials that will be worthy of your skills. You would not want the house or building you live in to be made with shoddy framework or a facade that will quickly start to show wear, or even worse, crumble.

CAMERA READY

These days the ability to take high-quality photographs is well in reach for just about anybody. Some online business owners have even found success using a good phone camera to take their product photography. If you are going to sell your beaded jewelry pieces, it is crucial that you have crisp, clear images of them. Using natural light is a great way to get flattering images of your jewelry. Early morning or late evening, about an hour before sunset, are good times to shoot in order to take advantage of the best natural light. You will want to avoid filters to give potential customers an honest impression of what their purchase will look like in person. Try to avoid cluttering the background of your images with props because this can be confusing for the customor to easily identify which item is being sold. Clean and simple is a good rule of thumb.

Have at least one photograph of each of your designs taken against a white or neutral color background. This style of photo is useful to share for any official purposes, such as for potential press or marketing materials. It is fine to photograph your jewelry in more of an editorial setting as well, whether on a model or flat lay, or both. These types of photos will help your potential customer imagine the item in their life. There are many photography classes and tutorials available, both online and in person. It's a great idea to enroll in a class or two if you want to take your own photographs, as it can make a huge difference in quality and increase your level of sales. If you want to hire a professional photographer, you can find one with reasonable rates by doing an Etsy or Google search, or checking local resources to find someone in your own town or city.

SELLING RESOURCES

There are many venues through which you can sell your jewelry online and offline. Here are just a few:

Etsy

Etsy.com is an established and popular online marketplace known for arts and crafts offerings, with a large presence of vendors who design and make their items by hand.

Ruby Lane

Rubylane.com is a high-end niche marketplace specializing in antiques and artisan jewelry.

Amazon Handmade

Amazon Handmade is a section devoted to handmade items on the online marketplace Amazon.com.

Your Own Website

Online marketplaces are a perfect way to get your feet wet and test receptivity to your work when you are first starting out, but at a certain point you may want to have your own website. This will allow you more control over your content, and you won't need to be concerned with the possibility of the marketplace going out of business or pay the fees associated with it. Many artists and designers choose to have both their own website as well as a presence on one or more marketplaces. Others decide to transition to simply having their own website. One advantage to remaining on a marketplace platform, in addition to having your own website, is that it will bring in a larger customer base that otherwise may not have known about your work.

Craft Fairs

Go online and do some research to find craft fairs locally and in surrounding areas where you can potentially sell your jewelry. You will find that some fairs are juried, meaning that not everyone who applies will be accepted. This is generally a higher quality venue where you may have a better chance of sales, though not always. Sometimes non-juried craft fairs at a local school, for example, can bring in a good number of sales. I recommend you do your homework. Attend a few craft fairs you're interested in selling at so that you can decide whether they are right for you. Pay close attention to the vendors who are there. Is the quality of their work similar to yours? Do the items offered seem original? Are they mostly from multilevel marketing brands, or cookie-cutter designs? Fairs that offer unique and good quality items will provide you with a better chance of your jewelry being seen by potential buyers who will value your work.

Once you find a fair you like, check the booth pricing and plan an attractive display (Pinterest is great for finding booth design inspiration). I have been able to grow my e-mail newsletter list at craft fairs by offering one of my necklaces as a prize to be given to a randomly chosen person. In order to enter to win, the fair attendees enter their names and e-mail contacts into a book I have placed next to the necklace. This is a great way to be able to keep in touch with potential customers.

Galleries and Consignment Shops

Research online to find local galleries, gift shops, and consignment shops. See if there is a section on the shop website stating who the buyer is (or call the shop and ask who is in charge of buying), and then e-mail them about the possibility of having your work offered in the shop. Include a photograph of your work embedded into your e-mail (not as an attachment) and a paragraph or two telling the buyer a bit about your pieces and what sets them apart from others. Ask for a short meeting where you can show them your work in person. Follow up with a phone call if you do not hear back within a week.

PROMOTING YOUR WORK

In addition to having excellent photographs when selling your work online, it is equally important that you develop your product listings and website (if you have one) for search engine optimization (SEO). SEO is the practice of writing your online product listings so they have the best chance of ranking higher in the platforms where they appear, whether this is a search engine, such as Google; an online marketplace, such as Etsy; or a social media platform, such as Instagram. One example of SEO is naming your photograph files with popular keywords (for example "silver_shell_necklace.jpg" or "opal_gemstone_ring.jpg"). There is a wealth of knowledge you can gain regarding SEO, and it is not a difficult practice to learn. You can find many online classes and books about SEO through a simple search.

Remember, wherever you sell your work, you will need to learn about and apply marketing techniques to promote it, and SEO is just one of these methods. Listing your jewelry in a marketplace or publishing your own website is just part of the work; equally important is letting people know that you exist. Set aside a little time on a regular basis, at least once a week, to work on SEO and other marketing tasks such as creating blog posts or posting to social media platforms, such as Facebook, Instagram, and Pinterest; Pinterest actually works more like a search engine and can garner excellent results. Choose just one platform to start and see how it works for you. You can add more later as time allows, though I would recommend no more than two or three platforms. All of this will help you get the word out about your work so that you can find more customers who will love and appreciate your gorgeous handmade jewelry!

Networking

Reach out to fellow artisans and designers and find out where they are selling their work. You can do this by joining a local artist business networking group if available. Don't worry if there are no groups available near you; join an online group (search for groups on Facebook and Google). Either way, you will have the opportunity to give and receive valuable information and make new like-minded friends!

Resources

ArtBeads.com

Everything needed to make bead jewelry, including great quality beads, stringing materials, charms, tools, and more.

Beadaholique
Beadaholique.com

Another online bead jewelry supplier offering a large selection of quality options.

BeadShop.com

Offers a smaller but still quite extensive and beautifully curated selection of bead jewelry-making supplies.

Beaducation
beaducation.com

Everything needed to create hand-stamped metal jewelry components including metal stamps, bench blocks, and mallets (which you will need for any hammered wire work). It carries other jewelry-making tools as well.

JoAnn
Joann.com

National fabric and craft retail chain. Visit its site to buy online or find locations near you.

Michaels
Michaels.com

National craft and hobby retail chain. Visit its site to buy online or find locations near you.

Nunn Design

nunndesign.com

Producer of quality American-made pewter jewelry findings. There are many inspirational photos and tutorials on its website, which offers mainly wholesale with a selection of retail items. Many of Nunn Design's items are available through the retailers listed on the site.

Raven's Journey

ravensjourney.com

Producer of authentic and gorgeous Czech glass beads. Visit its site for inspirational photos and to find retailers through which to purchase its items.

Final Words

This book was a labor of love, and I am appreciative of all the people who helped make it possible.

To begin with, I want to express my gratitude to my family for their continuous support and inspiration. Their love has been as a constant source of encouragement for me during this journey, and they have been my rock.

I also want to thank my friends, who have always been there to listen, give me guidance, and cheer me up when I've been down. Your words of advice and assistance have meant so much to me.

I appreciate everyone who kindly shared their knowledge and thoughts with me, including the experts, coworkers, and research participants. I owe you a debt of gratitude for helping to mold the concepts examined in this book through your contributions.

I also like to thank the institutions and groups who have supported this effort financially, with resources, and in other ways. Your support of my writing has allowed me to pursue my passion for knowledge sharing and writing.

Finally, I would like to offer my sincere gratitude to the book's readers. What inspires me to keep investigating and writing about these concepts is your interest in and engagement with them.

I want to admit that writing a book is not a lone endeavor before I end. It takes a village, and I'm grateful to have had such an amazing network of friends, contributors, and supporters. I want to thank you all for your significant work on this project.

Maisiej .X Powersk

Made in United States
Troutdale, OR
03/04/2024

18214306R00139